Advance praise for

WHAT TECH CALLS GOVERNING

"Daub is the consummate chronicler of Silicon Valley's autophagia. In this book, he shows it reaching its limit. A bracing exegesis from a wry and watchful observer."

—**QUINN SLOBODIAN**, coauthor of *Muskism: A Guide for the Perplexed*

"Daub traces Silicon Valley's transformation from imaginative force to dominant power, illuminating its increasingly troubling role in shaping politics and society. A lucid and important book that deserves a wide readership."

—**VEENA DUBAL**, University of California, Irvine

"One day, when the bubbles have burst and we are surrounded by the rusting ruins of the shiny new tech, we will look back on the clownish posturings of the Silicon Valley overlords and murmur quietly to ourselves, 'What a prophetic poke in the eye Adrian Daub gave them.'"

—**BRUCE ROBBINS**, author of *Atrocity: A Literary History*

"*What Tech Calls Governing* is sharp, engaging, and deeply researched. Accessible without sacrificing rigor or complexity, this book helps us decipher the strange and often contradictory messaging coming out of Silicon Valley. An invigorating read."

—**WENDY LIU**, author of *Abolish Silicon Valley: How to Liberate Technology from Capitalism*

"[Daub's] plausible description of that nasty blend of arrogance and immaturity—observable in the demeanor of tech bosses—explains very well why it is precisely such buffoons who have managed to attain ridiculous wealth and political power."

—**HARALD STAUN**, *Frankfurter Allgemeine Sonntagszeitung*

"Adrian Daub [delivers] a sober yet stimulating plea for the argument that technological dominance must always be inextricably linked with social responsibility."

—**BRANDAKTUELL.AT**

What Tech Calls Governing

WHAT TECH CALLS GOVERNING

ADRIAN DAUB

Stanford University Press
Stanford, California

Stanford University Press
Stanford, California

Library of Congress Cataloging-in-Publication Data
Names: Daub, Adrian, author.
Title: What tech calls governing / Adrian Daub.
Other titles: Was das Valley herrschen nennt. English
Description: Stanford, California : Stanford University Press, 2026. | Originally published in German under the title: Was das Valley herrschen nennt. | Includes bibliographical references.
Identifiers: LCCN 2026018278 (print) | LCCN 2026018279 (ebook) | ISBN 9781503648333 (paperback) | ISBN 9781503648340 (ebook)
Subjects: LCSH: Internet industry—Political activity—California—Santa Clara Valley (Santa Clara County) | High technology industries—Political activity—California—Santa Clara Valley (Santa Clara County) | Power (Social sciences)—California—Santa Clara Valley (Santa Clara County) | Elite (Social sciences)—California—Santa Clara Valley (Santa Clara County) | Masculinity—Political aspects—California—Santa Clara Valley (Santa Clara County)
Classification: LCC HD9696.8.U63 D3813 2026 (print) | LCC HD9696.8.U63 (ebook)
LC record available at https://lccn.loc.gov/2026018278
LC ebook record available at https://lccn.loc.gov/2026018279

Cover design: David Drummond

The authorized representative in the EU for product safety and compliance is: Mare Nostrum Group B.V. | Doelen 72 | 4831 GR Breda | The Netherlands | Email address: gpsr@mare-nostrum.co.uk | KVK chamber of commerce number: 96249943

Contents

Introduction

"YOUR AI AGENT NEEDS A WORKFLOW ENGINE."

The billboard stands by a nondescript stretch of highway somewhere between Redwood City and Mountain View. A boom, likely a bubble, made manifest. A cry of triumphant return. And probably one day, a monument to a bubble bursting. All hype seems destined to furnish tomorrow's ruin. But for now, this ruin in waiting stands by the side of Highway 101 to inform us that our AI agent needs a workflow engine.

Exactly 101 years ago, F. Scott Fitzgerald described a postindustrial wasteland on Long Island, "halfway between West Egg and New York," with a giant billboard towering over it, the eyes of Doctor T. J. Eckleburg. This stretch of highway may be less desolate than what Fitzgerald described, but the billboards seem just as unsettling and disconsolate as the unnerving, faceless eyes of the fictive Queens optometrist.[1]

Fitzgerald uses those eyes to find something sublime amid capitalist kitsch: the ephemera of consumer culture come to watch over and judge their creators, with the bizarre advertisement standing in for last things: God, fate, judgment, time. I too feel judged by "Your AI Agent Needs a Workflow Engine." First of all, because I had no idea, having left my AI agent lamentably bereft of a workflow engine. Second, because I don't even have an AI agent. And third, because I have no clue what any of it means. Like Rilke before the torso of Phoebus Apollo, I pass before the monument and get a sense that I am being told to change my life. Unlike Rilke, I have no idea what is wrong or how to go about remedying it.

The fact that this billboard poses an unremitting demand, but that even on repeat drive-bys I cannot for the life of me figure out what that demand is, says something about the company it's advertising. A company that, by the way, I have already forgotten. It says something about the place where a billboard could pop up by the highway. American billboards tend to be solicitous: they offer you a McDonald's, a world-famous geyser, a strip club, they tell you it's only five miles, and which exit to take to get to it. These are the least solicitous billboards imaginable, solitaires throning over the highway, haughty and without any desire to be understood.

And in this respect, this relentless sphinx feels like a perfect distillation of Silicon Valley in 2025. The billboard makes a demand without ever being able to clearly express what that demand consists of. This billboard seems to be telling a story about something entirely different: the fact that people no longer project onto this region what they once did, and that the region has therefore ceased to offer a screen for those projections.

This is by and large a new phenomenon. "What has happened to Silicon Valley?" is one of those questions that's so broad as to be unanswerable. To begin with, it's not entirely clear what we mean by Silicon Valley: a region? An industry? Those who've become famous for running that industry? What was part of "Silicon Valley"—in terms of geography, business model, or technological focus—was always, to some extent, a matter of the hype. Many companies wanted to be associated with it, even though, on closer inspection, they were quite traditional service providers, landlords, or real estate companies.

Silicon Valley was once the destination of choice for eager pilgrimages by neoliberal devotees from politics and the press. At the same time, it was a bogeyman for left-wing critics. Never entirely fictitious, but also never quite identical to the real tangle of office parks and suburban residential areas, of companies with corner offices and cleaning crews that stretches between Daly City and Cupertino along the San Francisco Bay.

Any attempt to answer the question, "What has happened to Silicon Valley?," will always be partial. But one partial answer might come from this unimpressive stretch of highway. And from the billboards that whoosh past as you head toward Palo Alto.

In recent years, the technology sector has extended its already dominant position. Almost all of the "Magnificent Seven"—the incredibly valuable tech companies Alphabet, Amazon, Apple, Meta, Microsoft, Nvidia, and Tesla—have more than doubled their market value in the last five years (in the case of Tesla, the market value increased by almost 500 percent, and in the case of Nvidia, by 1,300 percent).[2] While the market capitalization of these companies accounted for approximately 12 percent of the S&P 500 stock index in 2020, that number reached 35 percent in 2025.[3] The superrich among their founders had accumulated absurd wealth by 2010. Today, one would have to coin a superlative beyond absurdity to even remotely characterize their wealth. We live in a world of budding trillionaires, with payouts that exceed the gross domestic product of many industrialized nations.

Their political influence too has grown: In the 2010s, the major tech companies lived in fear of regulation; in the 2020s, they seem to have either checkmated the regulatory state or simply acquired it. Just ten years ago, SpaceX was offering its services to the US space agency NASA as a supplier. Now, it is well on its way to merging with the US space program. Thanks to the crypto boom and the AI hype, the companies' tendrils can now be found almost everywhere. Google was once exotic and far away. Today, the nearest data center or logistics hub is probably just a few highway exits away from where you are reading this book.

A staggering one million people work full-time in Amazon's warehouses. Five percent of all commercial structures built in the United States in 2025 were data centers, which are springing up everywhere. Excluding these data centers, US economic growth in the first half of 2025 would have been only 0.1 percent.[4] US media have almost entirely become subsidiaries of tech giants: CBS News belongs to the children of Oracle founder Larry Ellison, *Time* magazine to Salesforce CEO Marc Benioff, the *Washington Post* to Jeff Bezos, and *The Atlantic* to Laurene Powell Jobs. Whether it's Paramount Pictures or Time Warner, billionaires, and usually tech billionaires, pull the strings behind the scenes.

On the other hand, in a dialectical movement, Silicon Valley has lost its dominance in the realm of ideas. The further Silicon Valley colonized the world, the more its once uncanny ability to colonize the world's collective imagination diminished. The companies that once managed to appeal to both the left and the right found themselves forced to take a partisan political stance. Their founding figures had to align themselves with an emerging American fascism, a subservience that will tie their fates, to some extent, to the fate of Trumpism. And thanks to Trump's protectionism, these companies, which have always prided themselves on at least a superficial internationalism, must now position themselves as distinctly American companies—thereby running the risk of being drawn into trade wars.

Gone is the historic moment when every politician seemed to believe, or at least profess, that all you had to do was teach coal miners to code in order to guarantee full employment. Gone are the days when American politicians promised to "uberize" everything. Instead, we are now in an era when the CEOs of Alphabet, Amazon, Apple, Google, and even TikTok are having their pictures taken at Donald Trump's second inauguration; where Mark Zuckerberg is ingratiating himself with the Trump-supporting manosphere; where the restructuring of the government by Elon Musk, his Department of Government Efficiency (DOGE), and his ample supply of ketamine continues to affect what Americans can expect from their government; in which Donald Trump is attempting to prohibit states from regulating AI by executive order.

There was a moment when people readily confused men in turtlenecks with lapel mics pacing across a garishly lit stage with thought leadership. As a whole, we seem to have gotten better spotting that sort of thing as what it is: a pitch. Silicon Valley's ability to take over the world's collective imagination has noticeably diminished, in inverse proportion to its ability to actually take over our labor, our politics, our media. Silicon Valley's new innovations hardly get anyone excited, and they aren't presented to us as potential cult objects. If your new iPhone now comes with AI and your vacation photos are automatically compatible with the virtual reality headset you'll never buy, the tech industry has replaced yesterday's glittering promises with the exhausted air of neoliberal government—the shrugging acceptance of having no alternative.

In the last five years, companies have stopped promising us the world and are instead content to dominate it. Their power of persuasion has run out; raw power remains. Every story about Silicon Valley will always be incomplete. But this unassuming stretch of highway might offer a glimpse into how this happened.

I'm taking this drive with Wendy Liu, once a start-up founder, now a writer. And, like me, a long-term aficionado of these billboards.[5] I've lived in the Bay Area for almost twenty years, and for much of that time I've had to drive down Highway 101, which connects many of the towns and cities that compose what we call Silicon Valley. And for going on twenty years, the billboards by the side of 101 have been in the same locations. I don't recall many getting added, but I also don't think many have disappeared during my time here. At most, a few more have gone digital in the last fifteen years, their designs now exploring negative space in eye-searing HD rather than on good old-fashioned paper.

Successive waves of Silicon Valley hype have washed over these billboards, and then vanished from the earth. Ten years ago, the billboards overflowed with a cacophony of messages about e-commerce, customer relations management, chatbots, the Cloud. Then there was a moment in 2020, when they fell into disuse, when Silicon Valley—the region, as opposed to Silicon Valley the set of companies—seemed unsure of itself. Work-from-home became the new watchword, and the campuses along this highway stood empty. The shock of the COVID pandemic was global, but it chipped away at this region's self-image in a very particular way.

The region, the industry, and its billboards have recovered, and today they appear more triumphant than ever. And yet, as with so much that's currently making a comeback in the United States—Trumpism, oligarchy, white supremacy—one gets the impression that this isn't a more-or-less-normal swing of the pendulum. The boom, the bubble, the power that is currently swelling in Silicon Valley, and the ruthlessness with which boom, bubble, and power are presenting themselves by the side of this road, are more or less trying to equate themselves with the fate of the country, of humanity: if our bubble bursts, you, your planet, your future is going down with us. And so the billboards symbolize the fait accompli that Silicon Valley presents us with today: systemic relevance as an all-or-nothing bet.

In the 2010s, Musk promised us the moon: the Hyperloop, tunnel boring machines, an implant that would enhance our brains, the Mars colony. It was a fictional universe that rivaled Marvel or Star Wars. He delivered none of it. Nevertheless, he took over the US government. The supposed creators of yesterday have become the furies of destruction today; the prophets of disruption have become purveyors of "enshittification,"[6] and geniuses have become emperors in new clothes.

The dominance of corporations is increasingly tautological. We owe Elon Musk attention, we owe Meta our time, we owe OpenAI the use of its products, because it is simply our due. In 2025, Palantir CEO Alex Karp published *The Technological Republic*, his frontal attack on the declining self-confidence of the "Western world." The West has lost the belief in its own excellence—on campuses, through postcolonialism, through egalitarian state programs, through postmodern relativism. But tech companies, too, have lost their self-confidence, have gotten "lost in toyland," and have preferred to create consumer baubles instead of doing something real, where "something real" seems to mean either projecting power or helping the state project power.[7] For Karp, the fundamental problem of "the West" is that it no longer has an unproblematic relationship with its own dominance. We should be dominant because we are dominant. This is how Silicon Valley dominates today: simply because it does.

As an individual driver on Highway 101, you don't get the impression that these billboards want anything from you. These billboards are simply telling you how important they already are. Of the ninety billboards we pass during our drive, only about thirty have no connection to AI. The ones advertising AI are nondescript and interchangeable to a depressing degree. As Wendy rattles off what these companies actually do—background checks, website design, and (again and again) compliance—you get a sense of a crowded marketplace with very few ideas. "Wearable tech, shareable insights," reads one, promising "the AI data cloud." Saying that AI could have written that one feels generous. It reads like a bingo card.

"The current digital age," write Karp and his coauthor Nicholas W. Zamiska in *The Technological Republic*, "has been dominated by online advertising and shopping, as well as social media and video-sharing platforms."[8] This diagnosis seems outdated in the summer of 2025, just six months after Karp published it. It seems to me that the exact opposite is the case: hardly any of these billboards seem to want to sell me anything.

There was a time when tech took the effort to lie to you. The future it envisioned for you was undercooked and sketchy, self-serving and arrogant, but it was a future envisioned for you. The future imagined on these billboards is terrifying, and at best these billboards promise you might be spared that future. They don't tell you what you can do with their tech; they tell you what you can prevent. Six of the thirtyish non-AI ads promote the new iPhone, five have to do with customer relations management (CRM), one has to do with crypto. The rest: United Airlines, Coors beer, a NorCal casino, a steak house, and "Caring Erin", a divorce attorney. We both cheer when a billboard appears for Shen Yun, a dance troupe sponsored by a Chinese cult. At least it's not AI.

Besides Shen Yun, cults are markedly absent along this stretch of 101. The one thing you don't find here are the billboards churches put up elsewhere in the United States, with life-sized fetuses or demands to "Repent!" At the same time, the world depicted in these ads seems as grim as any doomsday preacher's.

Silicon Valley has returned, with fire and fury. It does not promise a world in which AI makes previously unimaginable things possible but a world in which only AI companies can protect you from AI. "You" in this case being the owner of a tech company, not a regular user, citizen, human being. For the rest of us, these billboards evince open contempt: "Who says hiring has to be fair?" asks a billboard for Metaview, "unfairly effective AI, built for recruiting." "Trust Humans" declares one Orwellian billboard for Checkr—a service that uses AI to run background checks on future employees, pitched at people who definitely do not in fact trust humans.

Of the ninety, only ten are for something that an everyday driver, even if they're quite wealthy, could possibly buy. Billboard after billboard is about things "you" need, which is only true if "you" happen to be a company with a hundred-million-dollar valuation. Ten years ago, these ads were already fairly targeted—not at the tens of thousands of drivers that go past them, but at a hundred of them at best. The remaining motorists get to simply be witnesses to some sort of pitch, some sort of seduction.

But those billboards weren't as inscrutable as the billboard seeking to impress on anyone driving by that their AI agent needs a workflow engine. That's what's so striking to an American used to being catered to by highway signage, to being guided, maybe seduced. These are signs that tell the driver that the message is not for them. "As a statement, it's so vague," Wendy Liu says. "They're sort of counting on you to be in the know. Or you don't matter." The next billboard just says "Caffeine," which certainly strikes me as a good idea. Wendy has to squint to figure out that it is in fact advertising a company called "caffeine.ai," which promises "the self-writing internet." Which, come to think of it, sounds like a threat.

Just as Fox News sometimes runs segments with exactly one viewer in mind (President Donald Trump), these billboards have a target audience that runs in the low double digits. For all their parochialism, these billboards stake a claim to the world. It's unlikely there are billboards for these companies anywhere else in the world, but these companies nevertheless claim world domination. They can justify their valuations only by promising to destroy not just your job, but your entire line of work. They can justify their high-flying claims only by strip-mining your posts, comments, photos. And they can scale only by building a gigantic data center near you, sucking up your water and polluting your air.

These billboards are claims to dominance, but those claims are not addressed to you. You are a mere onlooker to your own domination. There is something deeply unsettling about a power that seeks to justify itself but doesn't seek to justify itself to you. Such is the power of Silicon Valley. We can all opt out of caffeine, frame, C3.ai, and together.ai. Whether our opting out has any effect whatsoever is another story entirely. In many ways, witnessing the AI boom feels like driving along this forest of billboards: it's the dubious honor of getting to watch money fornicate with money.

Even Chevron's billboard along 101 is AI themed, emphasizing how many data centers run on burning oil and gas. Amid the glitter of solar panels to the left and to the right, the billboard is almost sneering in its petro-masculinist swagger: our AI is so important, we're feeding it your environment.

As you try to scan one inscrutable billboard after the other without crashing your car, you realize: these aren't meant for drivers. The person who'll peruse these and squint to discover the sponsor behind the nonsensical slogan is being driven in a ride-share, in a limo, or else in one of the shuttles that still dependably ferry employees to the big corporate campuses south of San Francisco. Except that it's hard to imagine a lot of shuttle riders looking up from their laptops to take in the flat, featureless landscape and in so doing start thinking "oh boy, my AI agent really needs a workflow engine."

No, it feels like these billboards are a sunk-cost fallacy given physical form. They appear to be here for people who have already invested, or are fairly certain they're about to invest. This is why they are so maddeningly withholding. That's why this advertising is so unbearably self-absorbed. For a long time, tech companies reveled in the role of outsiders, even when the basis in reality for this self-conception was rather thin. But the self-driving cars roll through San Francisco courtesy of subsidiaries of the Magnificent 7. And the AI ecosystem, through the practice of circular financing, resembles a fortified encampment: gigantic companies like Alphabet, Meta, Microsoft, Nvidia, and Oracle all own stakes in one another or are interdependent through licenses, for example, in data centers or chips. Here, too, the focus is no longer on catering to individual consumers or investors, but rather to the state. Because only the state could still save these companies if the sector were to implode—yet again.

The more I try to imagine the kind of person swayed by these advertisements, the more the group shrinks. I somehow doubt that someone working at one of the big venture capital funds, the ones that pride themselves on early access and unerring instincts, would bet on a start-up he found out about from a highway billboard. The real money in Silicon Valley is made well before anyone thinks to put up one of these garish monstrosities.

I begin to picture someone who works for one of the small "family offices," investment funds charged with increasing the fortune of a single wealthy family. When it comes to venture funds, family offices are often at the back of the line. A venture capitalist would much rather have a pension fund, a university endowment, or a sovereign wealth fund dumping billions into his accounts than a midsized family office. As a result, family offices often feel like they're on the outside looking in. I could imagine one of them looking at one of these billboards and thinking, "They're no unicorn, but at least they're an AI company." The investment world often operates with a distinction between "smart money" and "dumb money." But here it's probably more about early and late. The investor swayed by a billboard that simply says "caffeine" knows they're getting table scraps. Note that, in this image, our money doesn't even bear grifting. We're not eating. We see a billboard with the word "caffeine" on it, and drive on, borne ceaselessly into their future.

And that feels ultimately like what these billboards—like the faceless eyes of Doctor T. J. Eckleburg a hundred years before—are telling us about America's new Gilded Age: so much of our public discourse, so many of our vaunted institutions, so much of our collective attention, care, and heartbreak are sacrificed to the superrich conning one another. We can't understand what tech calls governing without the simple truth that it doesn't ultimately seem interested in governing us. What Silicon Valley calls governing is detached from and disinterested in human nature and normal life, even when it comes to normal life with technology and the internet. It is fixated on privilege and hierarchies for their own sake. And whatever intellectual ambition it possesses is easily seduced by ideologies that support these privileges and hierarchies.

This is not, or at least not primarily, about a change in the industry and the region we call Silicon Valley. It's about a change in our relationship to it. The problem is that because Silicon Valley has always presented itself as an image—and above all, succeeded as our image of itself—our evolving relationship with Silicon Valley has caused the Valley itself to transform. This predicament can also be described as follows: Silicon Valley has never adapted its theory of domination to its own dominance. What has changed, what has become more disillusioned and unremitting, is the gaze of those it dominates.

Being dominated here means being subjected to both actual power and ideological influence. Before Silicon Valley more or less took over those regulatory bodies in the United States that could have kept it in check, it hijacked the political imagination that could have done the same, that could have made regulation possible.

The C-suites of many iconic companies of the 2010s appear to have shifted dramatically to the right, conservative voices dominate among tech investors, the heads of the largest social networks have quickly caved to the new government. The tentative and often dishonest attempts to make the tech industry less male and less white are being rolled back all the more vehemently. And emerging fields like crypto and AI are dominated by voices ranging from hyperlibertarian to outright fascist.

The following eight chapters address what the title promises: The tech elite is in power, but what do they mean by power? It's about questions of authority, control, oversight, and dominance. Instead of examining these aspects individually, I will connect them to specific milestones in the development of modern Silicon Valley. My aim is not, or not only, to ask: What is the understanding of authority and power held by a Peter Thiel, an Elon Musk, or an ordinary venture capital investor?

It is primarily to ask how this understanding was developed. What schools, or schools of power, did Silicon Valley go through on its path to global domination? These schools are indeed widely dispersed: tech elites learned what it means to exert power in their families and at university, but also in gyms and on YouTube channels, in courtrooms and on their commutes. In their relationships with subordinates and service providers, fellow students, politicians, dominatrixes and sex workers. To ask "how do they exert power?" is therefore to retell the story of Silicon Valley as the apprenticeship of a fragile, and precisely for that reason domineering, masculinity.

As you drive, and watch the billboards singing each to each, knowing that they will not sing for you, you also notice that the dominance they project comes at the price of insularity. These billboards promise and demand the world, yet they seem to know less and less of it. "In the lives of emperors," Italo Calvino's narrator says in *The Invisible Cities*, "there is a moment which follows pride in the boundless extension of the territories we have conquered, and the melancholy and relief of knowing we shall soon give up any thought of knowing and understanding them."[9] We may be living in that moment.

ONE

Capital

When you walk across the Stanford University campus today, one thing that will strike you are the many names of famous tech founders gracing the various buildings, labs, and complexes. There's one named after Yahoo! cofounder Jerry Yang and his wife, Akiko Yamazaki; Bill and Melinda Gates are of course represented. Two buildings are named after Hewlett and Packard, and, fittingly perhaps, they sit directly opposite each other. The name that will likely catch your eye most often, however, is relatively unknown: Arrillaga.

The Arrillaga Family Sports Center includes a 16,000-square-foot weight room and the offices of the football program. At the Arrillaga Outdoor Education and Recreation Center, you can swim the Olympic-size pool or try out the climbing wall. The Arrillaga Center for Sports and Recreation houses the squash courts and basketball courts, and at the Frances C. Arrillaga Alumni Center, you can reserve a conference room and catering for your meeting. You can then burn off any excess calories at the Arrillaga Weight Room or the Arrillaga Tennis Center.

The money of John Arrillaga Sr., whose name is immortalized in the names of these buildings, is also Silicon Valley money. However, Arrillaga didn't found any start-ups, though he sometimes accepted their shares as rent. Instead, together with Richard Peery, another real estate developer, Arrillaga began in the 1960s to buy up gigantic parcels of former farmland in San Jose, Mountain View, Palo Alto, and Sunnyvale and throw up dozens of anonymous office parks—often without firm commitments or potential tenants. As the orchards and abandoned navy sites increasingly gave way to semiconductor factories and software companies, Arrillaga became enormously wealthy.[1]

It is, in a way, fitting that the most prominent donor to the university that embodies Silicon Valley like no other has nothing to do with software or semiconductors. Because ultimately, the university's wealth is also based on a strategy similar to Arrillaga's. Cynically speaking, Stanford is a tax-exempt investment fund with an attached educational institution and still by far the largest landowner in Silicon Valley.[2]

The power of "the Valley" may be new in many respects. However, the power from which this power derives is old. It results from social hierarchies, from land ownership and capital, and from the way in which both were exploited. And Silicon Valley's specific history of power creation influences the understanding of power held by those who became powerful here.

The Stanfords earned their fortune with the transcontinental railroad, particularly from government subsidies and contracts, which they, let's say, didn't always handle transparently. The estate, which today forms the campus, was their hacienda, the summer residence to which the family—Leland Stanford, his wife Jane, and their son Leland Stanford Jr.—could retreat. If, for instance, as author Malcolm Harris writes, the workers of San Francisco became too uppity, the Stanfords could withdraw to their little Versailles amid the California oaks.[3]

Unlike so many other US universities named after great benefactors, Stanford University was not the realization of a dynastic claim, but rather a monument to its failure, a catastrophe turned real estate.

Stanford is named after Leland Jr., who died at the age of seventeen a year before the university's founding. It still houses the young Stanford's mausoleum, and at the center of the enormous grounds lies Memorial Church, dedicated to Stanford Sr. In the early years, the path to the church led through a monumental triumphal arch, the Memorial Arch, with neoclassical reliefs befitting a Roman emperor. During the great earthquake of 1906, it collapsed and was not rebuilt. The campus thus preserves and perpetuates the rule of the Stanfords. But it is also evidence of a dynasty that never had the chance to develop. Above all, however, the Stanfords' only son and heir was immortalized in the name of the new institution: To this day, it is called Leland Stanford Junior University.[4]

When seen from the perspective of intergenerational transmission, this form of wealth transfer fittingly represents the region that grew up around the old hacienda. Freed from the vicissitudes of a mortal body and (until recently) from federal taxes, the Stanford heir lives on in his new guise as a university. Indivisible by the whims of family squabbles and immune to the decadence that would have likely befallen actual generations of actual, embodied Stanfords, Leland Stanford Jr. has ruled the area more effectively than any flesh-and-blood dynasty ever could. This seems to make the hapless Leland Stanford Jr. a perfect figurehead for an area where wealth possesses tremendous inertia and yet constantly changes and reinvents itself. Silicon Valley's power is also characterized by its habitual and arrogant refusal to question its sources.

Fred Terman was dean of the School of Engineering at Stanford from 1944 to 1958, and from 1956 to 1966 he served as the university's provost. These were arguably the most important years in the institution's history. After World War II ended, the US Department of Defense dramatically reduced its footprint in the Bay Area. The university struggled with its own marginality and was, in reality, little more than a stopover for ambitious researchers from the East Coast and a training ground for "the children of the middling rich of Los Angeles."[5] It was Terman who proposed establishing technology companies on the vast, largely undeveloped land of the Stanford estate. This led to the creation of the Stanford Industrial Park, now known as Stanford Research Park—usually considered the birthplace of Silicon Valley. Terman had the idea that the comparatively provincial university could flourish by trading on something it had in abundance: the Stanford family's land. Land ownership was transformed into company shares and rental income, and from these, into an endowment of more than forty billion dollars at last count.[6]

Together, these two incubators—the university and the research parks next door—have launched multiple generations of entrepreneurs. Surprisingly often, those generations have been understood as, and indeed presented themselves as, nouveau riche. In some cases, they were indeed that, biographically speaking. But the money that so reliably found its way to funding their sometimes bold, sometimes quixotic, sometimes fraudulent endeavors was old.

Today it comes from Saudi princes and Japanese banks. It comes from family offices that manage the real estate wealth or stock portfolios of American dynasties.[7] It comes from the endowments of universities established by America's kleptocrats. It comes from the "friends and family" of founders, from whom every start-up raises its first round of funding. Which means that far from opening up wealth to new entrants, the funding system actually highlights the opposite development: in the United States in general, and at institutions like Stanford in particular, the wealthy are increasingly keeping to themselves. And they manage to create wealth precisely by virtue of that fact. Silicon Valley is where chthonic cash is given the veneer of eternal youth.

Following the global financial crisis of 2008, many eyes turned to Silicon Valley. What these observers thought they saw there was somewhat paradoxical: the same old capital, but this time completely different. Everything was new, untainted. That novelty made the tech ecosystem legitimate and inspirational in ways that the rest of the economy, especially the banking world and the real estate sector, simply could no longer be in 2008. Homeownership and mutual funds had long represented forms of capitalism that could inspire Americans to dream, promising wealth and a rosy future and occasionally even delivering on those promises. After 2008, the promises of Apple, Google, and Facebook had to fill this void. This was all the more remarkable because the same region, the same industry, had already enjoyed a similar flood of excessive confidence several times before. In the media and political view from the outside, Silicon Valley somehow managed the trick of appearing new and untainted again and again.

In 2008, the tech industry was in a much better position to make bold promises than were other sectors because its promises had long drawn on the sector's potential for exponential growth. Discussions of the industry from those years invariably referred to Moore's law, which states that the computing capacity of integrated systems doubles, depending on the version, every eighteen to twenty-four months. Of course it is a "law" in the sense that those who build the circuits, as well as those who build things that use those circuits, rely on it as a rule of thumb in their planning for the future. In its application, Moore's "law" essentially required two things: The transistor capacity had to improve, and the companies making things running on them had to believe in the law. Silicon Valley owes its success not to the fact that it is an exception, but to the perception that it is an exception. The expectation of continuous profits, infinite exponential growth, an expectation that in other fields would be considered an indication of unseriousness or worse, has been a business principle here for decades.

In 2018, LinkedIn CEO Reid Hoffman coined the term "blitzscaling" to describe this understanding of the future, at a time when the scaling promises of many former start-ups had turned out to be something between hype and fraud. The difference between hype and fraud often simply depended on the mood of the investors. For many "unicorns"—start-ups that reach a valuation of over one billion dollars before going public—the expectations of enormous future profits haven't budged, even after twenty years of no profits. What has changed, in certain cases several times over, is where these profits, if and when they ever materialize, are supposed to come from.

Whenever a company fails to deliver the expected return, it is simply reinterpreted: "Actually," we are then told, it is not a transportation company, a rental platform, or a social network at all. "Actually," it's all about big data, the "app for everything," the blockchain, AI. Depending on which magic word makes the green light shine just beyond the bay—and makes the enormous destruction of capital in the present disappear from view: Musk's Boring Company will one day be incredibly profitable when it supplies the Mars colony operated by Musk's SpaceX with new living space using energy generated by Musk's SolarCity.

The success of many unprofitable companies in Silicon Valley depended on a capitulation of preestablished expertise. This situation could only arise because everyone—funders, regulators, politicians—refused to apply the logic of their respective fields to these start-ups. And they did so quite deliberately. The fantasy that these companies, this work, this form of capitalism was different from "normal" capitalism, that it was compatible with things that billionaires, venture capital, and massive profits are generally not considered particularly compatible with, proved remarkably enduring. One way of describing the disillusionment with Silicon Valley since around 2020 is: the corporations, their CEOs, and their products revealed themselves more openly as what they had always been: corporations, CEOs, and products. The only thing shocking is that a part of the public could still experience this development as shocking.

Silicon Valley dominates by converting power into other forms of power and by obscuring the obvious continuities between these forms. What neither Moore's law nor blitzscaling truly possess is a theory of dominance: How does dominance arise, and how does its mechanism manifest itself in reality? Kurzweil's singularity, the merger between human intelligence and machine intelligence, requires no coercion. It just happens somehow, at some point in the future. In truth, the leaders of Silicon Valley, like perhaps every nerd, did have such a theory. It was a theory of what they lacked, what they felt they were owed. As a result, it wasn't a particularly realistic one, but rather one based on science fiction and comic books. The CEOs embroidered it with their own moralism, combining power fantasies of the Muad'Dib from *Dune* or Hari Seldon from Isaac Asimov's *Foundation* series with another equally potent fictional narrative.

That narrative was Reaganism. The religious scholar Adam Kotsko has emphasized the theological aspects of neoliberal politics, pointing out that, for all its ostentatious appeals to rationality, the rhetoric of rationalization is not without its "demons."[8] Reagan's demons were students, "welfare queens," drug addicts, and people with AIDS.[9] Reaganism's others tended to be characterized by two things: On the one hand, the moral calculus of the 1980s emphasized self-control; it was terrified of permeability, loss, and waste. On the other hand, it depended on a preestablished harmony between what the individual deserved and what they received. It was animated by a concern that someone somewhere was getting something they were not entitled to, or that someone somewhere was not getting what they were by rights entitled to, which presupposes a set of hierarchies that are understood as natural but never explicitly named. Consider that in Reagan's language games, "taxpayers" never meant everyone who pays taxes, "citizens" never meant everyone who held a passport, and even "the people" seemed to exclude certain individuals who very much looked like people. In this view of the world, moral categories and hierarchies were (and in fact still are) simultaneously assumed and concealed. This mode of explaining the world has lived on in the way our tech overlords pitch their wares. In Silicon Valley's pitches, "everyone" has meaning only because it does not mean everyone.

This moral calculus matters in a situation in which Silicon Valley enters your daily life primarily through disruption. Joseph Schumpeter's concept of "creative destruction," on which the modern understanding of disruption is based, was intended to describe a morally neutral historical process. "Disruption," however, presents itself as amoral but is simultaneously hypermoralistic, because its acolytes love suggesting that systems, institutions, and even individuals deserve their disruption. It is the punishment for vanity, laziness, or the failure to heed historical signals of whatever kind. Thanks to disruption's latest avatar, "artificial intelligence" (AI), which currently dominates our news media, this imaginary punishment has shed the cloak of political theology and now appears quite simply as theology. That is to say: media discourses and tech

CEOs seem to turn to AI in a way a fulminating preacher once turned to the hands of an angry God.

Imagine it's the year 2015 and you work as a taxi driver. You feel the pressure that a company like Uber is exerting on your livelihood. You probably suspect that the company's business model is ultimately aimed at making someone like you superfluous and destitute. However, had you expressed this concern, the company and its stalking horses would neither have acknowledged this goal nor defended it as such. Instead, they would have defended the business model as an idea. You see, technological innovation unfortunately can bring about painful changes, they would have told you. Ultimately, it will lead us all—including you, the soon-to-be unemployed taxi driver—into a better, more efficient future. The new system will reduce emissions, enable autonomous driving, and, through the gig economy, integrate work more seamlessly into people's daily lives. We know that they would say this, because they trotted out all these justifications ad nauseam throughout the 2010s.

Now imagine it's 2025 and you are a university professor. You might feel threatened by the rise of AI. The same feeling as the taxi driver in 2015, but for somewhat different reasons. You feel threatened because the purveyors of AI are constantly and openly threatening you, and not with a shrug of the shoulders or vague gestures toward a better future, but with palpable schadenfreude. Large language models (LLMs) and other AI systems are destabilizing all sorts of ecosystems, companies, and professions; in fact, they currently seem to be destroying the job market for entry-level coders above all—and yet when tech leaders identify professional groups whose entire line of work AI will supposedly destroy, we constantly hear about authors, teachers, and "creatives." This isn't really because AI poses a particular threat to these groups. It's because the speakers believe these groups deserve impoverishment. "AI" is no longer the unintentional destroyer: It is the avenging angel of hierarchies that had been temporarily held in abeyance by others—the state, the parasites, the demons.

Fred Terman not only wanted to connect industry to the human capital of the university but also to connect new companies (many founded by his own students) to huge piles of money. Just a few years after the founding of the first technology companies in the area, like Hewlett Packard and Fairchild Semiconductor, Terman brought an industry to Stanford that has been a less flashy and less frequently acknowledged feature of the Valley's ecosystem: venture capital.

As the economist Tom Nicholas has pointed out, the American institution of venture capital (VC) emerged out of the attempt to ensure the persistence of capital amid economic windfalls connected to easily depleted natural resources, a monetary message in a bottle passed from one boom to the next.[10] In an economy geared toward the rapid exploitation of immense natural resources, VC was the way in which quickly earned money could be transformed into capital for the next boom. The great whaling families of New England secured themselves against the inevitable depletion of whale stocks with venture funds. And the railroad entrepreneurs, who had extracted enormous sums from the state, pooled their money to reinvest it for the moment when those subsidies inevitably dried up.

Today, venture capitalists are the central drivers in what tech calls governing. They are an integral part of the ecosystem, but a part that reaches both backward and forward, into a time before Silicon Valley and a time after it. The money they invest is of dynastic, sometimes even feudal, origin. The arrangement of this money with pluralism, with free competition, with liberal democracy is entirely provisional. This is something that those who manage it seem to sense acutely. Among the CEOs of the large technology companies along the San Francisco Bay, those openly sympathetic to the Trump regime are still in the minority. Among the venture capitalists, however, especially those you hear from in media, many are right-leaning.

Some, like Keith Rabois, have been active in conservative politics for decades. Others, like Marc Andreessen, can't seem to stop giving interviews about their drift to the right. Others yet, Chamath Palihapitiya (Social Capital) and Shaun Maguire (Sequoia Capital) for instance, long presented themselves as more moderate and even donated to Democrats—now they describe themselves as "red-pilled" and brag about their access to the Trump White House (in the case of Palihapitiya[11]) or how they worked on DOGE with Elon Musk (in the case of Maguire[12]). Multibillionaire Doug Leone, formerly a managing partner at Sequoia Capital, has been donating enormous sums to Trump's election campaigns for years. Peter Thiel's Founders Fund is almost a finishing school for right-wing to far-right members of the investor class. And thanks to David Sacks and Peter Thiel, it has now become a tradition that a venture capitalist delivers a tribute to Donald Trump at each Republican National Convention.

Whether these are exceptions or the rule, what matters is not the number of right-leaning VCs, but their style. In recent decades, it seems, the conservatives among them have developed a specific relationship to power, institutions, and community. These figures thrive on a hatred of the masses, but also strangely seek an audience that they don't require professionally. They live ensconced in wealthy enclaves like Atherton and Woodside yet are fixated on drug dealers on Mission Street in San Francisco and underemployed twenty-five-year-olds online.

Today the VC class dominates the United States, and yet its rituals are primarily about resentful retreat. Among the strangest of these rituals is VC Twitter. It's a truth universally acknowledged in Silicon Valley that venture capitalists, in possession of a certain status, must be in want of getting dunked on by twentysomethings on Twitter/X. They start posting everything that comes into their heads—the less thought-out, the more off-the-cuff, the better. Their vacuous emissions reliably attract (or attracted, before Elon Musk took over the platform) ridicule from ordinary users. There's something carnivalesque about these megarich, powerful men, who for not entirely comprehensible reasons put themselves in a situation in which people who are otherwise irrelevant to their lives make fun of them online. I once spoke with a young tech worker who in the 2020s attained some microcelebrity with her inspired and profane rants about sundry VCs and founders on Twitter. What astonished me at the time: a large number of VCs and founders followed her and interacted with her posts, as though lining up and hoping that this young woman might insult them next.

VC Twitter is legendary for obviously faulty logic, its ample dose of the Dunning-Kruger effect, its narrow-mindedness, and its silly air of self-congratulation. But above all, its tendency to escalate: These men (and they are 99 percent men) have a frightening amount of time on their hands. The posts fly back and forth at great speed, and it doesn't take long for a flurry of posts to fully lose contact with reality. "Will tweet as I wish and suffer the consequences," as the bio of founder Austen Allred, formerly head of the ed-tech start-up Lambda School, reads.

But the gentlemen seem to have their difficulties with suffering consequences, at least if they're the ones suffering them. At one point, the aforementioned young tech worker made fun of a particular billionaire in a tweet: "The human mind," she tweeted in November 2020, "wasn't meant to understand the sheer magnitude of how much" the billionaire was "a little shit."[13] Shortly afterward, her employer fired her. Quite likely because the billionaire had read the tweet. And was offended. And was an investor in her start-up. And was Elon Musk.

Although VC Twitter was given another shot in the arm by Musk's takeover, the year 2020 probably marked the high-water mark of the phenomenon. The investor class sat around at home, ordered food, and experimented with alternative therapies against COVID. And managed their cabin fever the way the rest of us did: by tweeting.

In August 2020, PayPal cofounder Keith Rabois tweeted that the American opioid crisis was actually China's fault. He provided no evidence for his thesis. A few minutes later, Jake Chapman of Alpha Bridge Ventures added the following reply: "Them shipping fentanyl to our shores is revenge for the Opium wars which 99% of Americans have never even heard of." A perfect piece of VC Twitter ephemera: a somewhat left-field brain fart that derived its rhetorical force from both its hallucinatory self-assurance and the fact that it positioned its speaker as smarter than "99% of Americans."

Only a little later, Austen Allred added another layer: "We're actually fighting with an enemy we don't even realize we're fighting. We're totally asleep, hoping they don't cross the Delaware."[14] On the one hand, the combination of unchecked self-confidence with glaringly little knowledge of detail in matters of Delaware-crossing is impressive. On the other hand, however, this communication is also the most normal thing in the world: three acquaintances from the same in-group who reinforce and try to outdo each other until the conversation yields essentially bombastic nonsense.

The "hot takes" of Rabois, Chapman, and Allred sit somewhere between posturing and genuine opinion, between big political pronouncement and in-group pandering. The whole thing reads like a completely normal chat conversation, with the one difference being that the three have a lot of followers on Twitter/X, which is why a kind of Greek chorus of users who weren't in the same bubble commented on each turn in the conversation with varying degrees of dismay. These investors naturally also have private chat groups, which are leaked to the public with some regularity, but here they toss their half-baked ideas back and forth in front of the rest of humanity. This semipublic dimension long gave VC Twitter its cringey fascination. At the same time, these men also seem to be craving reactions, of whatever kind, when they dash off their takes. Their tweets are currency between the men—and bait for everyone else.

For many of them, such rituals—and the public outrage—have long served community-building functions. In 1992, Rabois attracted attention at Stanford when he yelled in front of a professor's apartment that the "faggot" should "die of AIDS."[15] The stunt earned him a reprimand from the university—and the friendship of Peter Thiel. Shocking opinions strengthen these groups internally, giving rich, all-powerful men the feeling of being victims and underdogs together. The shocked reaction of the outside world is the currency with which young founders can then go to market. Conversely, if the reaction is less shocked and more sneering, they are capable of bottomless self-pity. It is probably no coincidence that it was among these investors that the idea first arose that perhaps one of their own, one who likes to trumpet big, barely substantiated takes into the world, might have to buy Twitter and silence those who mocked them.

Why didn't these VCs just stay away? Simply put, combusting into a gorgeous supernova of pure cringe on Twitter was part of the business model. These men made community through right-coded hot takes and indignant reactions once the Twitter mob went after those takes. One gained or maintained access to this particular social set primarily by letting oneself be bullied by ordinary users. The third musketeer in the aforementioned tweet thread, Austen Allred, was a favorite of the incubator Y Combinator; his start-up Lambda School (a programming school with a supposedly innovative payment system) was supported by various large VCs, even though the company had never been accredited as a school. In 2021, regulators became active, students complained about being ripped off, and half the workforce had to leave. The figures with which Allred had wrangled a valuation of one billion dollars (and thus the status of a "unicorn") from the venture funds turned out to be largely fictitious (in 2025, the company seems to be offering courses in AI).[16]

In the financial world, investigators sometimes speak of affinity fraud when a member of a particular group defrauds members of that same group, or when a fraudster exploits a group's social rituals to scam others. The reactionary tweets that VCs and their favorites like to put out into the world are dangerous for the social climate; however, they are probably intended as something else, namely, as a prelude to affinity fraud. The men who agree with one another online, or offer backup when someone comes under fire from normie wokescolds, are hoping for investments or the opportunity to invest. The reasons for this dynamic are manifold. VCs typically move in very small groups of like-minded individuals, where everyone is more or less like them or is hoping to be. Their tweets, as is so often the case in Silicon Valley, are not actually intended for you or me or other ordinary users, but are signal flares meant to attract the attention of investors and company founders.

Thus, the in-group of VCs and founders stands opposed and united against the out-group, which observes and ridicules their mating rituals. The tsunami of mocking tweets are merely a side effect. But such posts also offer psychological insights: VCs see their job as making quick but accurate judgments in quick succession. In reality, there is clearly a skill set that goes into picking out individual companies that might also appeal to other investors, in an industry flooded with capital. But whatever is part of that skill set, decisiveness wouldn't seem to be at the top of the list. Like so many in Silicon Valley, VCs are eager to see their good fortune attributed to merit, not to chance. Their job requires them to suppress the fact that VCs actually make endless series of decisions that, while making sense in the aggregate, are often foolish as individual decisions. It may be the most effective way of multiplying a petrostate's sovereign wealth, but you probably shouldn't be posting takes on social media like this.

However, VC twitter also stages a drama that Silicon Valley can't seem to get enough of more generally: the heterodox individual versus the herd. The ritual humiliation helps set a VC and his jejune opinions apart from the masses. It helps an individual get recognized by his peers as an outsider and a visionary, by being recognized by the general public as deeply silly. The sheer torrent of abuse also ensures that those whose lives an investor's capital will one day upend will, at least in his eyes, deserve it. By exposing himself to the ridicule of the masses, the naked VC becomes an emperor-in-waiting.

Something else is also striking: The takes with which VCs almost compulsively expose themselves to the ridicule of ordinary people can be about anything—dating, pop culture, genetics. However, they invariably find their way back to politics or leadership. Suggestions on how to recalibrate "the global economy," on how to transform San Francisco into a "network state," on who should be prevented from reproducing, on how to explain the high rate of homelessness in California. Their bets on various start-ups—at a time when low-interest capital was readily available and other investors were champing at the bit—have paid off often enough to compensate for the cases in which the investment completely evaporated or they fell for a scam. And from this success they derive a claim to shape the world.

Tim Draper is a third-generation venture capitalist. His grandfather, William Henry Draper Jr., was a banker and venture capitalist who, in 1959, founded Draper, Gaither & Anderson, the first VC firm on the West Coast. His father, William Draper III, left Draper, Gaither & Anderson in the 1960s and established Sutter Hill Ventures, one of the dominant VC firms to this day. Three of Tim Draper's children have followed him into the industry and now run their own investment funds. Which probably means that a Gen Z Draper is at most a few years away, itching to flood the world with money for AI start-ups and bizarre hot takes.

Draper's other hobby is dismembering the state of California. In 2013, he spent more than five million dollars to qualify a proposition for the California ballot that would have divided the state into six states. Another $450,000 went to political consultants. Instead of the California we all know and tolerate, there would now be Jefferson, Northern California, Silicon Valley, Central California, Western California, and Southern California. Yes, it would have meant that Silicon Valley would have had two senators of its own.

Most of the signatures needed for the referendum were procured by Draper's expensive consultants and proved to be invalid. In polls, broad segments of the electorate rejected the proposal. Ultimately, it was not even allowed on the ballot. Draper's pitch was: Every Californian would be able to choose their own California, and each California could choose its own "system." In 2018, he renewed his efforts, this time as a three-state solution. "We're trying to create states for the next millennium," he explained to Tucker Carlson, who was working for Fox News at the time. "The blockchain is changing everything."[17]

"Government is going to be completely different." Anyone who watched Draper campaigning for his Six Californias (or three, as in the 2018 proposition) beheld Silicon Valley's internal marketing jargon and the very real limits that jargon hits once it escapes containment. Blockchain, risk, choice, disruption—the tsunami of bullshit that had washed over Draper at every pitch meeting for decades had taken over, had poisoned his thinking. Like a St. Bernard, he faithfully retrieved the empty buzzwords and nonsensical advertising phrases that he and his colleagues tossed around when they were supposed to invest a Saudi prince's money in a new augmented reality start-up. Only he did so with absolute conviction.

Interestingly, the emptiest signifier in this endless stream of buzzwords was "government." Draper seemed to use this term in ever-changing ways: Sometimes it referred to the authorities that run a state; sometimes to the representatives one could elect; sometimes to the tax rate; other times to something like political culture; at times to constitutional structures, or a choice of "system";

then he was on to homeless people and drug dealers. There was no theory of governance behind Draper's proposal, merely a hodgepodge of complaints, of the kind someone would voice while skimming the *San Francisco Chronicle* in their villa in the hills behind Palo Alto. Sometimes he actually seemed to mean "governance," that is, the way governments make decisions and allocate resources. He accused California of being a "monopoly" because you couldn't move out of California without leaving California.

Whether right or left, in conversation with Fox News or local reporters, Draper's campaign was greatly handicapped from the start by the fact that its inventor couldn't really define the problem he was supposedly trying to solve. "I think that these three new states are going to empower people to realize what's possible in government," he told a skeptical-looking Tucker Carlson. "And then all these governments will realize that they can do a better job, and they can potentially compete with one another down the road for citizens."[18] He wanted to take power away from the established elites (among whom he, a third-generation venture capitalist, a graduate of Stanford and Harvard, for mysterious reasons did not count himself). He wanted to empower Californians, without saying what that power consisted of.

He didn't seem to notice that a touch of elitism was at play when an insular billionaire wanted to realize some pipe dream and turn upside down the lives of forty million people. If you looked closely, Draper of course wanted to govern, to rebuild the state according to his idiosyncratic ideas. But for him, the quintessential venture capitalist, governing was always something that others did; he positioned himself as an outsider. He was merely a provider of money and talking points. The fact that Draper was actually addressing problems that primarily affected the superrich like himself—in other words, that the main beneficiaries of his proposal would be people who own property in several Californias and could choose their own tax regime—didn't seem to occur to him.

It was a perfect example of tech industry "solutionism": A solution put forward for a problem that nobody could recall actually having. A pose of problem-solving that seems to have but a distant connection to the problem it supposedly solves. Draper explicitly promoted his project by pointing out that his bets on the future had made him rich: He mentioned an early investment in the Chinese tech giant Alibaba. An equally early investment in Theranos, one of the most spectacular fraud cases in Silicon Valley, had apparently slipped his mind.

Let's assume the referendum on "Six (or Three) Californias" had been successful. Let's assume the federal government had agreed, and so had the other states and the president. Would the three- or six-state solution have turned out to be an Alibaba? Or rather a Theranos? You can invest using a scattershot approach, but you can't govern that way. Governing requires decisions, and while Draper clearly saw himself as decisive, he was actually someone who instinctively kept his options open. That's how he makes his money, after all.

In 2024, when many in Silicon Valley openly supported Donald Trump, Draper was the exception. Six (or Three) Californias would have been a great gift to the Republicans—the name of the northern Californian state "Jefferson" was an explicit reference to a far-right attempt at state formation in the border region between California and Oregon. In 2024, however, Draper made a Solomonic decision, endorsing both Kamala Harris and Donald Trump. Which meant that no one could follow his endorsement without immediately invalidating their ballot.

What manner of shaping the world was the six-state solution? On the one hand, it had the audacity of a radical political project, but on the other hand, it pretended to be prepolitical, primarily concerning how politics will eventually be conducted in Jefferson, Silicon Valley, and West California. It clearly had a political bias and stemmed from dissatisfaction with the Democrats who dominate in real-world and unitary California. However, the proposal shied away from positioning itself in terms of party politics. Carving the left-leaning Bay Area and Los Angeles County out of California is a dream that Republicans in the Golden State have harbored for years. But Draper seemed to genuinely consider his proposal nonpartisan.

This is the form of dominance characteristic of the tech industry. Dominance is presented as a given, obvious and legitimate. At the same time, dominance is being frantically disavowed because it might risk coming with actual responsibilities and consequences. What is more: the understanding of dominance that Draper presented somewhat clumsily was a natural consequence of his business model. Six (or rather, Three) Californias was a pitch. The justification for his undertaking was disruption; Draper didn't feel the need to provide any further explanation.

After the failure of his ballot initiatives, Draper did not react like an entrepreneur who had pitched an investor but had left empty-handed; instead, he retreated into a sulk. It couldn't possibly have been due to the marketplace of ideas, where his idea had simply failed. No, the fact that no one actually found anything appealing about the idea was a sign of its brilliance: For Draper, the failure was "another example of the dysfunction of the current system," which "underscores the need for six new, modern governments."[19] The reason Draper was so dismissive is a fundamental one: The Californians who would have had to put the referendum on the ballot and then give their approval to the proposal were not, in Draper's world, the funders, but the customers. There was simply no place in Draper's worldview for the sovereignty of those people in California whose expression the new Californias were supposed to represent.

TWO

Vibes

Silicon Valley is very taken with the "vibe shift"—a neologism describing a change in the prevailing sociocultural mood. Sean Monahan coined the term in an essay on Substack. He primarily meant for this societal climate change to apply to music, pop culture, and coolness. But Silicon Valley thought leaders who have always been a bit out of touch when it comes to music, pop culture, and especially coolness, quickly applied the term to politics: "Wokeness" was out, right-wing radicalism was in. The wealthy right-wingers of Silicon Valley were quick to appropriate the neologism for themselves. Marc Andreessen proclaimed it "the vibe shift" when, for example, Peter Thiel gave a presentation on cryptocurrencies at Bitcoin Miami 2022.[1]

These days, in the United States, Silicon Valley—long criticized by conservative forces as a stronghold of "wokeness"—is instead being hailed as the supposed antithesis of, and indeed corrective to, everything conservatives currently despise. The leadership of many zeitgeist-shaping companies from the 2010s has indeed shifted dramatically to the right; conservative voices predominate among tech investors; the CEOs of the largest Silicon Valley companies have embraced right-wing ideology or have submitted to government bullying. The halting and often dishonest attempts to make the industry less male and less white are being rolled back with much less hesitation.

When right-wing culture warriors targeted DEI (the acronym stands for diversity, equity, and inclusion), Alexandr Wang, then CEO of Scale AI, announced a "MEI" policy as a counterproposal—merit, excellence, and intelligence. Making the point, in case you missed it, that supposedly "diversity" and "excellence" are contradictory. In emerging fields like cryptocurrencies and AI, positions ranging from hyperlibertarian to outright fascist set the tone.[2]

The empirical evidence behind Monahan's diagnosis of the "vibe shift" and Andreessen's adoption of it is fairly weak. People with above-gerbil powers of recall might remember that very similar diagnoses were made in 2016/17, though back then they were made about the alt-right. But the important thing about the vibe shift isn't whether it exists or not. What's important about the vibe shift is that Silicon Valley (or a certain part of it) believes it's real. As so often happens, what initially presents itself as a neutral analytical category turns out to be primarily a self-portrait. Silicon Valley believes that the wind has shifted in the world because the mood has shifted in parts of Silicon Valley, and because Silicon Valley has long been unable to distinguish between itself and the world. It feels as if there are a thousand launches, and behind a thousand launches, no world.

The history of the present is, to a large extent, the history of self-radicalizing elites. And if diagnoses of the "Vibe Shift" are at all relevant, it is because they provide an involuntary self-portrait of such a radicalization process. For all its global influence, Silicon Valley can be surprisingly small and provincial. The creators of our filter bubbles have long resided in the mother of all filter bubbles. The richer the CEOs became, the smaller and more uniform their bubble seemed to become.

In 2020, the investor Paul Graham wrote an essay titled "How to Think for Yourself." One lesson: "If you're surrounded by conventional-minded people, it will constrain which ideas you can express, and that in turn will constrain which ideas you have. But if you surround yourself with independent-minded people, you'll have the opposite experience: hearing other people say surprising things will encourage you to [*sic*], and to think of more."[3] At the end of the essay, Graham thanks the broad panel of independent thinkers with whom he has surrounded himself: Six of the seven are men between forty and fifty-five years old. Five of the seven work at Y Combinator, a business incubator in San Francisco cofounded by none other than Paul Graham. One is the CEO of the payment service Stripe. The seventh is Peter Thiel.

The difficult thing is that at the very moment when the world seemed to be adapting to Silicon Valley, the region itself was changing. While the world was still naively gaping at the apparent wonders of Silicon Valley and the question of how to replicate the model it seemed to offer was omnipresent, people often overlooked that this was still a very specific backwater looking to remake the world in its provincial image.

The unmistakable rightward drift of many of the industry's leading figures is likewise often attributed to global factors: to the government in Washington, to wokeness, to capitalism, to the globally ascendant illiberalism. Yet much of what has changed in Silicon Valley can be chalked up to dynamics within the Silicon Valley region itself. The companies are, after all, based here; for a long time the CEOs lived in three or four zip codes and met in ten or fifteen overpriced restaurants with ten or fifteen of their closest clones.

A myopic perspective on the world has long characterized the tech industry, but success has amplified it. Age and wealth often inhibit contact with people whose lives and careers have unfolded in fundamentally different ways. When great fortune befalls an individual, they might ask themselves some lonely nights: "Do I really deserve all this?" But when a group collectively rushes from success to success, when truly extraordinary success has become the norm by the age of twenty-five, thirty, or thirty-five, and you are forced to then age alongside one another for decades, each constantly aware that your peak lies ever further in the past, then it helps when fellow travelers constantly reassure you that you are still relevant, that the gnawing feeling of irrelevance is, in truth, the fault of others. A concept like "vibes" allows them to understand their aging process, and the alienation that inevitably accompanies it, as identical to the course of the world.

In such a social set—highly networked, very homogeneous, completely fixated on other members of the same group—the mood can shift very quickly indeed. People say that Silicon Valley has moved to the right, but it is doubtful whether significantly more employees of Meta or Google voted for Donald Trump in 2024 than in 2016. But Trump's supporters among Silicon Valley CEOs and billionaires did act differently in 2024 than in 2016, and they did feel they were speaking for more and for different people. We know that the tech giants are behaving differently when it comes to the second Trump administration than they did when it came to the first. That's the vibe shift that matters. Whether Silicon Valley detected the changes in the rest of the world like a seismograph, or whether Silicon Valley primarily listened to itself, the future will tell. In any case, the drivers of the New Economy are the driven of the Even Newer Economy.

The past few years have made obvious, even spectacular, the reactionary streak, the faith in natural hierarchies behind the disruption rhetoric and bad-boy posturing, the male dominance politics behind nerdy social phobias. The years since 2016 brought #MeToo and Black Lives Matter. But also the COVID measures, which deeply offended the sensibilities of the tech oligarchs because they allowed the state to flex its muscles and strengthened the bargaining power of the workforce.

Although unions are still a rarity in Silicon Valley, forms of organized solidarity among tech workers have become increasingly common in recent years. The "Google Walkout," a protest against unequal treatment and sexual harassment of women in the workplace, became particularly well-known. On November 1, 2018, Google employees initiated a global strike, which traversed the globe from the company's offices in Tokyo all the way to the mothership in Mountain View. The company found itself having to respond to the globalized anger of its workforce. And although governments continue to treat Silicon Valley with kid gloves, since the Cambridge Analytica scandal involving election manipulation there have been a few antitrust cases and hearings in the US Congress that the government had previously refrained from pursuing.

Anyone who wants to witness an ur-scene of the Silicon Valley elite's rightward shift could do worse than to watch a recording of a 2018 US Senate hearing. Zuckerberg had to sit before the joint Senate Judiciary and Commerce Committees for hours answering questions; he looked crestfallen, like a student being summoned to the principal's office. Above all, it must have become clear to him how few friends Facebook had in Washington then: Republicans were angry with him, Democrats were angry with him, which in a two-party system is a rather unpleasant position to find oneself in. Much of Zuckerberg's erratic course since 2020 can be understood as an instinctive escape from this experience. He wants to avoid at all costs ending up where he was back then. He wants to escape the control of the state, the control of a civil society he seems to picture as feminized and nanny-ish, the ire of a woman like Elizabeth Warren.

That's because Republicans criticized Zuckerberg based on more or less hallucinatory conspiracy theories, claiming their freedom of expression was being suppressed. These accusations were ultimately cosmetic, and Meta managed to deal with them relatively easily over the years. The criticism from the Democratic senators, especially that of Elizabeth Warren, went to the heart of Meta.

"If someone's going to try to threaten something that existential," Zuckerberg said in 2019 in an address to staff, which was leaked to the tech portal "The Verge," "you go to the mat and you fight."[4] Zuckerberg the fighter was born. A year later, the pandemic hit, and Zuckerberg began training in mixed martial arts and jujitsu.

At the same time, however, the inherent dynamics of the tech industry brought the founders' long-latent hierarchical thinking to the surface. Once upon a time the disruptors didn't need to argue openly in hierarchical terms because they were already at the top. Then Silicon Valley's obsession with disruption ran up against its real limits. The proponents of disruption did not handle it well at all and consistently blamed not their own thinking but rather the real limits.

One of these limitations simply consisted of the inertia that comes with being a newly dominant company like Alphabet or Meta. How plausible is your claim to disruption and heterodoxy when you are as established and professionalized as your average multinational oil and petroleum concern? Another limitation was that those who had once been disruptors have themselves become the target of disruption by rebellious outsiders. The best they can still manage is to acquire promising newcomers (as happened with autonomous driving) or to copy them (as happened with AI). Until recently, cars from Uber and Lyft were everywhere in San Francisco. Often enough, the drivers were former cabbies, whose old profession had been destroyed by the rideshares. By 2025, Uber and Lyft are as rare as taxis in the city, and the self-driving electric cars of Google subsidiary Waymo or Amazon subsidiary Zoox dominate the streetscape.

Instead of confronting the new competition, for example from TikTok, or acquiring it, corporations like Meta have resorted to using national security arguments to persuade the state to eliminate the competition. The same companies that had positioned themselves as libertarian against the state began to identify their interests with those of the state. The enormous investments in AI have a leveling effect: companies that have always thrived on being the first are one after another joining a pack of multi-billion-dollar lemmings. The fact that they can do this is an indication of their dominance. The fact that they use their dominance in this way, however, is a sign of evident weakness.

In precisely this respect, these companies' alliance with MAGA was also somewhat organic: like Trump, whose special trick has always been to merge an addiction to dominance with a feeling of his own inadequacy, weakness and strength have fused in a strange way in these companies over the past five years.

It was a time of enormous economic, cultural, and political dominance for Silicon Valley. However, the corporations have collectively become alienated from the very region with which they once publicly identified. Many of Silicon Valley's leading figures no longer officially live there. Many have staged their break with their former adopted home in a highly publicized manner, sometimes repeatedly. Whether it's Elon Musk's move to Austin or Peter Thiel's repeated moves to Los Angeles and later to Miami, the break with Silicon Valley, the break with San Francisco, the break with California is always a media spectacle. Apparently, once you reach a certain level of wealth, you can't leave the area without quickly giving a few interviews about homeless people and tents under highway off-ramps. Palantir cofounder Joe Lonsdale has been sponsoring the Cicero Institute for years, which specializes primarily in prohibiting homeless people from sleeping on the streets. In November 2020, Lonsdale announced that he would be moving with his family, his venture capital fund, and the Cicero Institute to Austin, Texas.

These superrich individuals complain about homeless people and tents in areas that they probably only know from pictures on Twitter/X. Because what you quickly realize when you actually live in the region is that when it comes to billionaires, the statement that someone lives here, or is moving here, or moving away from here, is often more or less metaphorical. In 2024, Mark Zuckerberg sold his estate in idyllic Woodside, where Larry Ellison, John Doerr, and Joan Baez also live. At first, no one noticed, since the property simply changed from one limited liability corporation to another for almost thirty million dollars. A moving van was either never parked in front of the house in Woodside, or it was there constantly.

The situation was similar at Zuckerberg's villa on 21st Street in San Francisco, which he sold in 2022. Today, the only thing that tells you about the former owner is the fact that this house is the only one on the block that is pixelated on Google Maps. In total, Zuckerberg owns a real estate portfolio worth three hundred million dollars, including a large part of a Hawaiian island. The only indication that Marc Andreessen no longer lives in his $27 million estate in Atherton, an even more upscale suburb right next to Menlo Park and Palo Alto, is that one less resident is fighting against a law that would require the town of Atherton to finally allow multifamily housing.

The departure of billionaires is just as ambiguous as their presence once was. On the one hand, these self-proclaimed exiles from Silicon Valley are still very much around. Musk staged his move with great fanfare, but soon he was back in town and, at least in his telling, slept on a mattress in the Twitter headquarters on Market Street. Despite several moves, Peter Thiel still seems to show up with great frequency in San Francisco. In what sense, then, is San Francisco "their" city? When they come to the region now, are they here as locals or as governors? And were they ever locals? Even now, when they are probably less frequently there, they are by no means less dominant. In fact, they dominate the city almost more as *dei absconditi.*

People often speak of the "exodus" of tech executives from San Francisco. But for an exodus to occur, you first have to have been there. Their claim to being locals was usually in their leaving. In April 2023, Bob Lee, the founder of Cash App, was found stabbed to death in San Francisco on a deserted street in the shadow of the Bay Bridge. In the following days, tech executives outdid each other on Twitter and in the media in complaining about the decline of the city—which most of them had officially already left.

The politicization of the murder began with a tweet from a far-right former wrestler and Twitter influencer from Miami. "A good friend," he wrote on Twitter/X, "was murdered simply while walking down the street." And he added: "Fuck San Francisco." As is typical with right-wing content on X, CEO Elon Musk quickly discovered the tweet and boosted it, commenting: "Violent crime in San Francisco is terrible." This was the starting gun for a collective nervous breakdown among the tech right.

The venture capitalist David Sacks speculated on the podcast "All-In" that the perpetrator was "a psychotic homeless person."[5] Musk weighed in to tag in San Francisco's DA, calling for "stronger action to incarcerate repeat violent offenders."[6] When a San Francisco police spokesperson warned against jumping to conclusions, angel investor Jason Calacanis lost his temper: "EVIL INCOMPETENT FOOLS & GRIFTERS WHO ACCOMPLISH NOTHING EXCEPT ENABLING RAMPANT VIOLENCE," he wrote on Twitter.[7]

Ultimately, it turned out that Bob Lee had been the victim of another tech entrepreneur whom he knew personally. After a party at the exclusive Millennium Tower, Lee had voluntarily gotten into the BMW of an IT consultant whose sister he often partied with. A long-simmering dispute seems to have escalated, leading to the murder. A crime of passion involving drugs, ambitions, and elite parties. Anyone familiar with San Francisco knows that there are three blocks between the Millennium Tower and Lee's hotel. Had he walked, he would probably still be alive today. Lee thus likely fell victim to precisely the alienation from the city of San Francisco that later shaped the reactions to his murder.

What was interesting, however, was not just how instinctively the city's wealthy sought the culprit among the city's poorest, how readily they identified people like themselves as victims and people who, by all logic, were actually their victims, as potential perpetrators. Even more interesting was how readily Sacks, Musk, and Calacanis reclaimed residence in San Francisco when it came to badmouthing "their" city. (Although Calacanis admittedly didn't officially leave San Francisco until 2024.)

Once Sacks, Calacanis, and their colleagues gathered on their podcast after the arrest, they had—once again—identified the victims: themselves. "We got all these reporters, who are basically propagandists, claiming that crime is down in San Francisco," Sacks complained. (Crime was down in San Francisco.) "They are all seeking comment from me this morning . . . and trying to dunk on us."[8] Their prejudgment of a city they had all since turned their backs on wasn't prejudice, Sacks insisted, "but logic." These men's will to dominate increased with distance. And it increased the more abstract and vague those whom they dominated became for them. The more it became about "logic," rather than lived experience.

In their rush to call for state intervention while simultaneously complaining about the slow grind of institutional justice, one notices something deeper. These men are alienated from political decision-making because their entire theory of dominance requires traditional political decision-making as its foil.

The form of innovation for which the rapidly scaling companies of Silicon Valley became famous in the 2010s worked only because regulators react more slowly than technology develops. The profit margin of a company like Uber consisted of the gap that existed between something technically feasible and its, more or less inevitable, legal regulation. This has changed in recent years—whether crypto, autonomous driving, or AI: companies are starting to make regulation impossible from the outset and then developing technologies that can fill the gaps they have created. Only sporadically does it occur to them that they are thereby neutralizing their opposite pole. When they call the police in San Francisco. Or a taxi.

The rhetoric of tech companies has changed. In particular, tech companies' relationship to reality has changed. This process began in California during the 2020 pandemic year. Instead of the power of persuasion that once came so easily to this industry, the industry was increasingly concerned with getting others to simply acknowledge its power and accommodate themselves to it.

The COVID pandemic is one of those historic experiences that almost all people worldwide went through, but which, depending on the region, country, and social class, they likely experienced very differently. How did this experience manifest itself in Silicon Valley? COVID was a feeling of collective powerlessness. In Silicon Valley, where people have difficulty with both collectivity and powerlessness, the pandemic was perceived as an unparalleled affront, even a humiliation. Many of the ultrawealthy founders and investors of the region reacted to the staggering speed of the virus's spread, and to the rapid measures taken to thwart it, with two contradictory impulses: They minimized the crisis, compensating for the feeling of general loss of control by convincing themselves that they knew better than everyone else, yes, better than the virus; and they hyped themselves up, convinced that their technology would fix everything.

When COVID forced the United States into lockdown in March 2020, the tech companies reacted with a slew of proposed solutions. But notably, they were the kinds of solutions they proposed whenever anything needed solving. Their proposed fix was to collect people's data, or to get them to download unnecessary apps. The reaction of Silicon Valley's superrich coupled activism with cynical self-enrichment, and they used the pandemic to criticize government, while engaging as little self-reflection as humanly possible. The sector approached the pandemic with its characteristic "solutionism"[9]—that tendency to misunderstand complex social problems as a series of easily solvable technical problems. Everything was half self-promotion, half misunderstanding.

On Twitter/X, Musk's disciples begged their idol to "invent" a miracle cure for the virus (preferably in collaboration with Bill Gates). Musk seemed flattered by the tributes offered to him. At the same time, he was desperate to swim against the current, which tends to make leadership difficult in times of crisis. And so it happened that Musk, on the one hand, promised quick solutions and, on the other hand, tweeted like a second-rate blogger, that "the coronavirus panic is dumb."[10]

Peter Thiel's big data play Palantir suddenly touted its own software as a means for contact tracing. The investor Shervin Pishevar made headlines for organizing a fleet of two hundred 3D printers that were supposed to produce "ventilators and masks." The billionaire Tom Siebel gathered a group of tech luminaries around him to deploy "money and AI" against the virus. Elon Musk promised to procure ventilators for California hospitals. Tim Draper boasted that, "while old methods were flailing on creating a cure, it was the company Verge Genomics, a Computational Biochemistry company that determined which FDA approved drug would be the best treatment for Covid-19."[11]

If you don't quite remember any of this, it's because solutionism hit some firm limits at the beginning of the pandemic. Much of what Silicon Valley promised was, at best, opportunism, a pitch, and a publicity stunt. At worst: incompetence. The Valley primarily perceived the unprecedented crisis as an opportunity to once again beat the drum for itself and implicitly belittle the state and its capabilities. Verge Genomics, a biotech start-up funded by Y Combinator, did indeed have a drug for amyotrophic lateral sclerosis in its pipeline—a possible cure for the new virus. As fate would have it, however, the key did not quite fit the lock. The 3D-printed masks apparently never materialized. Musk really did send material to California hospitals—what arrived at the hospitals, however, were respiratory therapy devices used to treat sleep apnea, but crucially not COVID-19.[12]

The medical breakthroughs that more or less ended the pandemic came from the FDA and the pharmaceutical industry, not from Y Combinator. In the end, it was the experts from international organizations, and various levels of the government who enabled a return to normal.

But while they were feigning responsibility, even statesmanship, the elites of Silicon Valley also gave in to their opposite impulse: to isolate themselves, to buy their way out of collective fate. While Peter Thiel tried to convince governments to adopt Palantir's contact tracing technology, many in Silicon Valley's executive suites were more interested in his free-trade islands, the "seasteading" project. Ultimately, no billionaire actually moved to sea, but many fled to bunkers or remote estates, particularly in New Zealand.

In general the pandemic intensified the tendency among CEOs to offer grand pronouncements about the state of the world—whether they dismissed the pandemic Trump-style as a "hoax," understood it as a doomsday scenario, or (as in most cases) both at once. Marc Andreessen used the pandemic as an opportunity for a general reckoning with "the West" and its "institutions". "Every Western institution was unprepared for the coronavirus pandemic, despite many prior warnings. This monumental failure of institutional effectiveness will reverberate for the rest of the decade," he wrote in April 2020.[13] On the surface, Andreessen's essay was a fundamental critique, but it seemed to exempt Silicon Valley, or at least people like himself, from this criticism. In fact, the crisis, at least according to those in Silicon Valley, only served to confirm Silicon Valley's own self-image.

Tim Draper once again predicted the age of blockchain—once the lockdowns were lifted, he wrote on Twitter, the dollar would effectively have already been replaced by Bitcoin. For many entrepreneurs in the Bay Area, the intervention of the city and state was a shock. But above all, it came as a shock to those among them who were no longer actively running businesses but were instead cosplayers pretending to be entrepreneurs. CEOs who were already retired, former founders who spent their days playing tennis and hanging out on Twitter.

In 2020, this was true for most of the prominent CEOs or VCs, whether it was Bezos or Draper, Andreessen or Sacks, or Thiel. Even Musk, despite his restless energy, was a super-senior pretending to be a freshman. They no longer had to go to an office with strangers every morning, and yet it was extremely important to them that others should please go to the office to hang out with strangers every morning. They reacted with incomprehension to the fact that the government was quite generous in enabling work-from-home arrangements. In their libertarian moral calculus, they had bought their way out of worry and fear of death. The fact that (some) others should now no longer be plagued by worry and fear of death, although they felt was morally those people's lot, seemed to them an injustice. That was their fundamental experience of COVID: They perceived being the same as others as persecution, as an upending of the moral order of the world.

After some initial turbulence, the pandemic led to a veritable boom for the tech industry. The region around the San Francisco Bay had earlier and more effective lockdowns than other parts of the US. This kept the death toll very low, but it continues to affect the area. In particular, the superrich in this region seem never to have gotten over the lockdowns. They felt as powerless as the rest of us, but they also felt disempowered in more specific ways, which has affected their understanding of power in general. And so the lockdowns in Northern California are now shaping the reality of life in far-off countries. The fixation on regulation is nothing new in Silicon Valley. But the relationship with the government was severely affected by COVID.

The attempts by Silicon Valley CEOs to seize control of the reins of state intensified around that time. Moreover, this historic moment influenced what they wanted to control in the first place. They understood the government only in terms of what they could see of it, what affected them in their entrepreneurial activities or their daily lives, or during lockdowns: the existence or absence of regulation, employee protection, and a sense of security.

After all, many a CEO experienced COVID as a humiliation at the hands of their own workforce. Musk was obsessed with the "stupidity" of the COVID measures because they affected his Tesla factory in Fremont, across the Bay from Palo Alto. In spring 2020, Musk waged a bitter battle with Californian regulators, including Governor Gavin Newsom, because he wanted to keep his factory running. "Tesla is restarting production against Alameda County rules," Musk announced via tweet on May 11, 2020. "I will be on the line with everyone else. If anyone is arrested, I ask that it only be me."[14]

The tweet shows how strongly these weeks in the spring of 2020 shaped the politics of the following years: the CEO is supposedly "on the assembly line" and offers himself as a sacrificial lamb for his workforce, when in fact he's making them risk exposure to a dangerous virus. The CEO plays the populist, but actually disregards the will of the people, putting ordinary workers in great danger. And he casts those who try to prevent infections and advocate for the interests of his employees as the villains. Of course, Musk was never "on the line"; he just tweeted that he was. In other words: Musk's revolt against California regulators in 2020 is structurally indistinguishable from how Donald Trump governs in 2026.

Even today, the home office trend shapes the inner city of San Francisco. The office vacancy rate in the city was, until recently, enormous; only thanks to the AI boom does the situation seem to be improving somewhat. During the heyday of home office, one tech company after another closed its office tower in the city or decided to cancel headquarters that had already been announced.

I remember visiting Dreamforce in 2022, a trade show that the software giant Salesforce holds annually in SoMa (South of Market). Back in the day, almost 100,000 people in polo shirts and sneakers thronged the downtown area for Dreamforce. In 2022, there were perhaps 30,000 people strolling along the Astroturf on Mission Street, which had been specially converted into a forest, or past the gigantic murals teeming with cartoon wildlife. Attendees were listlessly bagging sundry promotional items. The halls of the Moscone Center were deserted, while a handful of bored ushers played Candy Crush on their phones.

Salesforce offered me an interview with a woman from their board of directors—presumably for lack of other takers. She was absolutely wonderful, and to her the palpable lack of energy wasn't a big deal. The company culture wasn't focused on presence and performance maximization. This made sense to me, because the company was making a fortune thanks to services like Slack.

Nevertheless, the interview couldn't resolve a central contradiction for me: On the one hand, Salesforce has a strong connection to San Francisco—the enormous Salesforce Tower is still the tallest building in the city and dominates the skyline; the Salesforce Transit Center is a huge transportation hub where one day, if it ever materializes, the high-speed train to Los Angeles will begin its journey. Pandemic or no pandemic, the company still wanted to capture the hype, the energy that comes with a developers' conference, wanted enthusiastic participants for the video spots and a festival atmosphere for the young programmers.

But of course time hadn't stood still for the young programmers. They had had their first child in 2018, had moved to the East Bay during the pandemic, and enjoyed being able to take the kids to school together, thanks to work-from-home, Slack, and Salesforce. Or the programmers were single parents, cared for sick parents, had a disability, or came from far exurbs and could never have afforded San Francisco. Especially during the employment boom during the latter stages of the pandemic, the social makeup of internet companies had changed. Salesforce had gone along with this change and had become highly profitable because of it—and yet here the company was having trouble adjusting to the new reality its products shaped. For many others, these shifts scratched at their cherished self-image far more painfully.

Certainly, similar disruptions also occurred in other industries and at other locations. However, in no other industry are these disruptions likely to have undermined the self-image—at least in the minds of the C-suite—as much as in the tech industry. During the pandemic, the workforce had broken the companies' social contract, which stated: There is no social contract. The CEOs of Silicon Valley had long relied on a vocabulary that declared their companies were not conventional companies, and had put pressure on their employees with this rhetoric.

Now, these employees suddenly behaved like perfectly normal employees. They preferred working from home, stayed away from the endless team-building exercises and all-hands meetings, refused to come to the office, were allergic to unnecessary risks, and fiercely defended the privileges they had won. Worse still: In both the last year of the first Trump administration and the early Biden era, the workforces had the state, especially its regulators, on their side.

Who knows, perhaps another state would simply have tolerated the antics of Elon Musk, who sought to continue production in his factories undeterred. California, on the other hand, adhered to the laws and made no exceptions for alleged geniuses. The alleged geniuses never forgave the politicians for this.

Add to that the problem of institutionalization. Another shift, perhaps less clearly discernible to the outside world, is that companies today are more aggressively and directly steering the fate of the region than they were ten years ago. The dominance of the technology industry in Northern California long seemed somewhat unintentional. When Google shuttles made it impossible for ordinary citizens to reach their bus, when a start-up wiped out restaurants, laundries, or similar businesses, when charming diners and dive bars gave way to overpriced coffee shops, or when tech bros manipulated the reservation system for city soccer fields, they were often bewildered when confronted with the consequences of their actions. That's not how it was meant at all! They often didn't acknowledge the influence they had. Or if they did, it was as an unintended by-product of their success, for which they didn't think they could be blamed.

By now, they identify more strongly with their own power. They openly acknowledge the hierarchies that they previously dismissed as outdated, or as not quite applying to the world they claim to want to create. They behave like a perfectly normal elite. This can be illustrated by their relationship with the universities, and especially with the house university of Silicon Valley. For a long time, one had the feeling that the university was chasing after these men—vying for their attention, wanting to prove itself to them—while they seemed to only sporadically take notice of it.

But this pose, even if it was just a pose, changed. Silicon Valley regained interest in the university, so long as it was one that simply replicated what they were already doing. Starting in 2016, Peter Thiel began co-teaching a class on sovereignty in the Department of German Studies. Thiel had given the university, which he had attended from 1985 to 1992, a scathing review in his book *The Diversity Myth*. For years he was most famous for paying young people not to go to college. Now he wanted to teach, wanted the institutional imprimatur, so long as that approval didn't come with the need to actually engage with the field or institution he was joining.

Laura Arrillaga-Andreessen, daughter of megadonor John Arrillaga and wife of venture capital billionaire Marc Andreessen, was meanwhile allowed to teach at the business school. When these somewhat strange arrangements eventually expired, it became clear that it had never been about a partnership, but rather an attempted takeover. Marc Andreessen went on the warpath against the university. In a chat that was leaked to the *Washington Post*, he fumed that they had "driven my wife out of Stanford . . . a decision that will likely cost them something like five billion dollars in lost donations in the future."[15]

It would be wrong to say that men like Thiel or Andreessen dominate Stanford more today than they did ten or fifteen years ago. The university has long been dependent on wealthy, often right-wing libertarian and reactionary alumni. And far more than from their money, the university naturally benefits from their prestige. But the example shows: The mode of dependence, the form of dominance, has shifted in recent years.

Men like Thiel or Andreessen have developed a finer sense of what the world supposedly owes them. They have a more concrete understanding of what domination means to them. Empirically speaking, talk of disruption, genius, etc., remains ubiquitous. The reactionary elements in the tech discourse have merged with reactionary politics in the broader sense—a politics that today routinely uses language that ten years ago would have been more likely to be found in TED Talks than in politicians' speeches. This means that this way of thinking has shed its ideological character; it has revealed itself to be what it always was: a form of governmentality. This way of thinking alters the flow of information, power, and responsibility within governmental structures. This governmentality preserves its supposedly libertarian ethos only for those at the top—for everyone else, it creates structures that could be described as either neofeudal or authoritarian.

THREE

Dominance

One of the characteristic pathologies of our age is that we find it difficult to distinguish between discursive and political dominance. No one claims that discourse on social media exerts no power. But how did it come about that, in diagnosing our historic moment, we attach more weight to individual tweets than to the statements of the owner of Twitter/X? The currency of our present is attention; to capture and direct it is one important form of power. The superrich—and especially those hailing from Silicon Valley—are in the process of taking over and openly influencing all major US media outlets. Yet we get upset about people arguing incorrectly on social media.

Sarah Wynn-Williams's book *Careless People* tells the story of Facebook in the years 2011 to 2017, roughly the period in which the platform, especially among members of my generation, dominated the lives of countless millions. According to Wynn-Williams, however, within the company that era was characterized by erratic political amateurism and a lack of interest in the political framework and dimensions of the business model.

In scenes that rival the work of Larry David in terms of sheer cringe comedy, Wynn-Williams recounts stories of heads of state who don't even get past the lobby at Facebook because Mark has an important meeting with the programmers.[1] And conversely, she describes Zuckerberg's brief visits to summits, where he stands around awkwardly and no delegation wants to talk to him. Wynn-Williams presents all of this with a sense of humor, but she also sees a certain tragedy at play. Facebook was enormously influential politically, and neither Zuckerberg nor the heads of state seemed to take this influence seriously enough. What she doesn't say: Only when the app lost its obvious anchor in everyday life, when the platform lost its market dominance, did the company start digging its claws into politics.

This makes a certain amount of sense. Many early employees came to Facebook because of the technical challenges. People like Wynn-Williams, who comes from the world of diplomacy and had to invent her role in the company, were exceptions and, accordingly, outsiders at the company headquarters. Wynn-Williams and others like her sought to articulate the political opportunities and dangers that came with the large platforms early on. For their bosses, the vocabulary of making the world a better place was, at best, an awkward second language.

Stories like Wynn-Williams's contain an important point about the dominance of Silicon Valley: it is fundamentally unreflective. It takes itself for granted; it does not question itself. Taken for granted in several respects: The image of dominance that those currently in power have is fueled by a barely digested course of reading and opportunistically misunderstood philosophy. But it is also important to realize that these people grew up to rule the world. Granted, the levers of power they sit at today did not exist when they were children. But nevertheless, the levers of power, whatever form they might take, were practically handed to them at birth. Our tech elite wields power with the self-assurance of the privileged and with the ignorance of those who feel disempowered—a fatal combination.

The dominance of the tech elites derives its strength from a lack of understanding, from disinvestment. Our tech elites, and their mode of governance, does not understand the things they dominate. And our elites largely confront this lack of understanding not with shame, but with a perverse pride. It is the perfect way to exercise power in the age of elite populists. After all, deriving the legitimacy of your rule from the fact that you've barely spent any time trying to understand the thing you're running is a discipline in which Elon Musk and Donald Trump manage to be world class.

Yes, this form of domination reshapes the functions of the state. When ignorance becomes the lingua franca of governing, it has to be adopted even by those who actually know better. Thanks to Donald Trump and Elon Musk, Washington, DC, is now exactly as a few venture capitalists and some college dropouts from Silicon Valley long perceived it. In the summer of 2025, Donald

Trump's Treasury secretary, Scott Bessent, told CNBC that the Federal Reserve, whose interest rate policy Donald Trump disliked, should be brought to heel. "All those PhDs over there, and I have no idea what they're even doing. It's kind of like a universal basic income for academic economists."[2]

Three things are telling about Bessent's remark: First, the idea that Bessent presented his professed lack of understanding as an asset rather than a flaw. Admitting to "having no idea" was intended as a brag. This is the cardinal error of Musk's disruption fetish, only that Bessent wasn't threatening to blow up a rocket, but the global financial system. Second, Bessent's statement was widely seen as an application for the position of Fed chair. His statement that he didn't understand the Fed was supposed to increase his chances of being appointed to run it. This is the political theology of the age of disruption: ignorance is purity, expertise is sin. And third, Scott Bessent has been working as a financial manager for years. Of course, he knows what the economists at the central bank do. He's not an ignoramus, but he was playing one for his boss.

The economist and former Greek finance minister Yanis Varoufakis argues in his 2024 book *Technofeudalism* that we have left capitalism behind and that the global economic system has entered an entirely new phase of development. Varoufakis describes a system in which more and more people are dependent on platforms that control their labor, to such an extent that they can render this labor unsellable with a single click. Whether we agree with Varoufakis from an economic perspective, "feudal" seems a good description of the strange combination of control and indifference with which the rulers, precisely thanks to highly advanced technological capabilities, now view those they govern.

Palantir Technologies is a good example for this combination of control and indifference. Founded in 2003 by Peter Thiel, Alex Karp, and Joe Lonsdale, the company is an explicitly conservative undertaking, driven by explicitly conservative men. Its techniques of statistical analysis of vast, often nonpublic databases (data mining) are primarily tailored to the work of the police, the military, and other repressive state apparatuses. Palantir is highly controversial. Whether Palantir can deliver on what the company promises is questionable. In the imaginations of those warning about Palantir, the company becomes the highly capable, almost preternatural data miner, in other words exactly how Palantir presents itself to potential customers.

This doesn't mean it's wrong to warn people about Palantir. But our warning shouldn't focus on what the company's tech can do. Our warning should concern the fact that that tech is deployed at all. It simply doesn't matter whether

Palantir's newfangled systems are more scarily omniscient than the old ones. If the people to whom this technology is applied include undocumented immigrants in the US or Palestinians in the Israeli-occupied territories, then it is almost immaterial whether the algorithm picks out the "right" people. Those in power have already decided that there are essentially no "wrong" targets in these groups. Palantir is necropolitics, pure and simple.[3] The data sets are merely window dressing. It's not the fact that the data miner might miscategorize someone that makes an individual a victim of Palantir, but rather the fact that Palantir is categorizing them at all.

The shift I am describing is not primarily related to real economic and political power. It is worthwhile to keep in mind the French theorist Louis Althusser's description of ideology as "the imaginary relationship of individuals to their real conditions of existence."[4] Regardless of whether we are actually entering a completely new phase of economic development, as Varoufakis suggests, it is clear that the perspective of those whom Varoufakis positions as feudal manor lords has changed with regard to the real conditions of their—of our—collective existence.

Elizabeth Holmes founded Theranos in 2003. The company, which claimed to have developed special devices for the rapid and accurate performance of blood tests, was a sensation in the late aughts and early 2010s. But by 2015, the start-up began to collapse under the weight of fraud allegations. When it did, in October 2015, Elizabeth Holmes gave an interview to Jim Cramer, the host of the television show *Mad Money*, to defend herself. "First they think you're crazy," she told Cramer, "then they fight you, and suddenly you change the world."[5]

But what exactly was "the world" that was supposed to be changing? Holmes later repeatedly returned to a proposal to change the way in which the FDA approves and monitors blood tests. The problem, she argued, was that regulation in the health-care sector was slow to adapt, not that the innovative power of start-ups could give rise to flimflammery. Cramer criticized her for many things in this interview, but not for this claim. Holmes seemed to be suggesting that, if her machines violated regulations, the fault lay with the regulations, not with the machines. Specifically, Holmes was likely referring to a report from the FDA, which described the company's tiny blood containers as an "unapproved medical product." However, as Holmes well knew, the lack of approval was not the main problem with the containers, which in reality appear to have been encrusted, foul-smelling mini blood volcanoes.

Changing regulation and innovation, at least in Holmes's telling of the tale, stood in an ambiguous relationship: Was she saying that her innovation would change the world if the regulations were adapted? Or did she mean that the world had to change so that her innovation could be considered innovative? The point is: The question whether the tests that Theranos offered could do what the company claimed they could do is easily answered. No, they could not. But what Holmes presented to Cramer was something else: the imaginary relationship that Althusser describes. Not: Can the machine do this? But rather: How must we restructure our understanding of government, of accuracy, of either having diabetes or not, so that we can convince ourselves that the machine could do it?

This strange modality often comes into play when our chief technologists design a future in which normal people—who either have diabetes or don't, and who would like to know which is the case—are relegated to being mere spectators of their own future. "Space represents hope for many people," Elon Musk once wrote on X. Musk's space fantasies, however, are based on the exclusivity of space: hope, certainly, but only for a very select few. Silicon Valley CEOs have been referring more and more compulsively to the representation of hope and the future in recent years, rather than to specific hopes or futures. For a very simple reason: the hope and future they are talking about are no longer those of the people living today or their children. They exist in some fantasies of long-termism or effective altruism; we, the 99.9999 percent of humanity who don't run a tech company, appear in these people's dreams, if at all, as noise.

In November 2020, Californian voters approved Proposition 22 with 55 percent of the vote. California's propositions allow voters to bypass the legislature, and in many cases the courts, to establish law, tax rates, and regulation directly. Proposition 22 established that gig workers were free agents, not employees of the companies on which they depended for their livelihood. In this, the proposition contradicted the extensive research into the economics of gig work: while some may pick up gig work as a side hustle, as time goes by the activity begins to look more and more like a traditional job, and what is more, the companies themselves have mechanisms—loyalty and support programs, algorithmic advantages, etc.—that seem designed to shuttle drivers or workers along in this development, to make them more and more into regular employees in all but name.[6]

In a landmark ruling two years earlier, the California Supreme Court had determined that gig workers were employees under certain state laws and not, as the companies contended, "independent contractors." A law, California Assembly Bill 5, from 2019, was passed to address this ruling. The campaign to get Californians to pass the ballot measure, which cost the major delivery services Uber, Lyft, and DoorDash over $200 million, essentially made the same suggestion as Elizabeth Holmes had in her desperation in 2015. What if the opposite were true? What if the world adapted to our standards instead of us adapting to theirs? The California Assembly Bill and the California Supreme Court had recognized something (certain gig workers) as something (employees). Proposition 22 was nothing less than the suggestion: What if we didn't recognize this thing for what it is, but rather for what it isn't?[7]

Ten years ago, Uber would have argued differently, emphasizing flexibility, climate, and efficiency. All of that was gone by 2020. Proposition 22 embodied a corporate supremacism. "Prop 22" wasn't about persuasion; it was about getting voters to acknowledge the power of tech companies, to react to that power, and ultimately to submit to it.

One could describe this as a variant of Hegel's dialectic of master and slave. A very specific form of technology discourse has begun to shape and even dictate our reality, but at the expense of its descriptive power. It no longer acknowledges reality, but only because it is content to merely shape it. This is—and this is Hegel's point—both a sign of strength and a sign of weakness, a sign of dominance and a sign of inferiority. If, rather than focus on the contradictions in what Richard Barbrook and Andrew Cameron once called the "Californian ideology,"[8] we pay attention to the violence with which it seeks to dominate, we quickly arrive at Hegel. For Hegel concepts were our tools for reaching out into the world and seizing it. But the threadbare appeals to disruptive rhetoric and the aesthetics of genius are like a cat desperately trying to dig its claws into a wall to keep itself from falling. Its convulsive attempts fail and are, precisely for that reason, particularly violent.

The book in which Hegel tells the story of master and slave is the *Phenomenology of Spirit*. This means that master and slave are figures of consciousness; they each represent elements of human experience. In Hegel's argument, the division of labor between the two figures is eventually made impossible by the respective content of their divergent experiences. The master decides how things are named, while the slave deals with the buzzing, blooming confusion of existence and experiences its difference from the official description. "That consciousness, *qua* worker, comes to see in the independent being [of the object] its *own* independence."[9] The master does not attain a corresponding insight.

This seems to me an accurate description of what is happening today: Yes, a very specific Silicon Valley ideology prevails and rearranges the world according to its own self-understanding. At the same time, the incongruity between this ideology and the way things present themselves to the rest of us is becoming increasingly obvious. Proposing that this absolute dominance brings about its own downfall is not meant as a kind of utopian point. I mean it rather to explain something else: The impotent rage of which our new technofeudalism is capable, despite, or in tandem with, its ever-increasing power, is an expression of the fact that this discourse describes less the more it dominates.

Disruption names a very specific form of dominance, most centrally one of the outsider. According to its own self-understanding, it originates at the periphery of a system. What disruption does to this system is somewhat ambivalent: On the one hand, it destroys it; on the other hand, it also preserves it. It tends not to destroy the supply chains, the cycles of our economy altogether, but of course ruptures individual links, individual nodes, along the way.

Above all, however, disruption as a gesture and self-image is irresponsible in the deepest sense of the word. Disruption does not see itself as responsible for what it dominates. It derives its legitimacy from the demonstrative nonacknowledgment of responsibility. "Move fast and break things" was once the slogan in Silicon Valley. In the United States, 2025 marks that historic moment when this form of dominance merged with the business of government.

Certainly, politics had long since accommodated itself to the fetish of disruption, but now disruption was used to collect taxes and run schools. Whether we look at the bizarre cuts and shakedowns of Donald Trump's second term in office, the flimsy justifications for the tariffs he introduced and then suspended, or the stochastic purges carried out by Elon Musk's Department of Government Efficiency: they all employ the language game of disruption; indeed, they are inconceivable without the disruption fetish of the last ten to fifteen years. For they are all guided by the idea that disruption represents a proven antidote to established interests, ossified structures, and the pieties of professionalized elites.

That DOGE ultimately attacks a specific group of employees, who are also conspicuously often neither white nor male, and mysteriously leaves the privileges of the superrich untouched (for example, in the defense budget or the tax code), is not particularly surprising. What was not yet so readily apparent in 2020 is the fact that these purges would be only half-heartedly sold as efficiency measures. In the hands of Musk and his coterie of college dropout henchmen (such as Edward "Big Balls" Coristine), they mutated instead into a form of redemptive violence that—entirely in the spirit of techno-fascism—was touted as a purification of the body politic.

DOGE's efforts—outside of its name—were only superficially based on the language of efficiency. Rather, they drew from three semantic fields: (1) DOGE promised an end to the parasitism Musk allegedly encountered everywhere in the federal government but that often seemed to consist only of his inability to correctly read an Excel spreadsheet. (2) DOGE held out the prospect of destroying conspiratorial and illegitimate "elites," specifically the "Deep State." (3) Its representatives dedicated themselves to pushing back against "wokeness," to saving American institutions from the "virus" of the civil rights regime. What tech calls thinking is often highly compatible with fascism. "Disruption" was always the name for this compatibility—the point where economic dominance, political fixations on purity, and fantasies of annihilation could merge seamlessly.

The college dropout, the outsider, the nerd have long shaped the popular image of Silicon Valley. The dropout has on the one hand has contact with the elite and the institution (any dropout we care about was once at a prestigious college), but has also publicly renounced this contact (the dropout did not graduate and claims not to need a degree). Many of Silicon Valley's intellectual stalking horses have become somewhat threadbare as a result of ten years of media oversaturation, but the dropout continues to thrive.

The figure has always had its dark side. But thanks to DOGE, the popular image of "the dropout" (as opposed to the tens of thousands of kids who drop out of universities for an endless number of reasons) has become completely demonic in 2025. DOGE consisted mostly of a band of college-aged kids who five years ago would have built a mediocre app and become rich with it, who instead became a government agency in all but name that laid off cancer researchers en masse and shredded the social safety net. The image of the college dropout is changing. After about thirty years convincing ourselves we've met Dr. Jekyll—Jobs, Zuckerberg—we now get "Big Balls" as Mr. Hyde.

In the semantic field of "disruption," experts and technocrats with decades of experience are pitted against youthful, rebellious energy that sees what the experts don't. It is a semantic field that is, by nature, quite versatile. You can claim that young, audacious rebels shake up the system by replacing expertise with logic for pretty much every field. It is a theodicy of rupture, a logic that says that every form of destabilization is good, that every system deserves to be shaken up from time to time, and that it is morally good to discomfit the mandarins. This contrast is all too familiar to us from other industries and sectors. However, its application to governance seems to have surprised many Americans.

No one was quite so primed to apply this logic to government as an administration whose officeholders across the board perceive themselves as outsiders, as standing outside governance. RFK Jr. clearly sees his job less as administering the Department of Health and Human Services and more as disturbing how it is normally administered. Perhaps this is because Trump and his hangers-on instinctively sense the same thing Silicon Valley's evangelists of disruption sensed: that this form of dominance is not the same as governing. What Americans are learning now with respect to their government is that irresponsibly assuming responsibility is tantamount to a regime of sheer nihilism. What Americans may not have noticed: how long they ignored this nihilism when it presented itself as the ideology of the tech industry.

There were clues: When Silicon Valley imagined dominance, this contradiction emerged with remarkable regularity. Peter Thiel and Alex Karp named their surveillance company Palantir Technologies after the Palantíri, the "seeing stones" in J. R. R. Tolkien's *Lord of the Rings* that allow powerful wizards to gaze into distant lands and even into the future. Yet, Tolkien's trilogy seems to operate with a more complex theory of power than the company executives who reference him.

Certainly, the Palantíri are enormously powerful artifacts in *Lord of the Rings*. But in the plot of the trilogy, we encounter only one such stone, and it seems to represent precisely the opposite. Saruman the White sees through the stone exactly what the Dark Lord Sauron wants him to see, and is thereby corrupted by evil. Tolkien thus uses the Palantíri as a motif in the same way as the Rings of Power: technologies and techniques of empowerment that all too quickly transform into a form of enslavement.

So why name a company after such an object? And, while we're on the subject, why name a company that sells thick protein shakes after Soylent Green, the all-purpose food in the film of the same name, which is famously made from the processed remains of the elderly? Why do those who most eagerly promote AI constantly talk about the technology as if it were Skynet from the Terminator series? The identification with dystopia is striking. There is a canonical tweet from 2021 about this mechanism:

> Sci-Fi Author: In my book I invented the Torment Nexus as a cautionary tale.
>
> Tech Company: At long last, we have created the Torment Nexus from the classic sci-fi novel Don't Create The Torment Nexus.[10]

Certainly, this ready identification with villains, often totalitarian villains, is already plenty creepy by itself—and also explains the large personal and ideological overlap with an administration dominated by online Nazis, who often like to draw inspiration from cinematic heavies. But there is also a fundamental poverty at the heart of an ideology that gets excited about fictional dystopias, villains, and totalitarianism. Not because those are evil, but because they're usually so thinly drawn. The fact that we always see these cinematic villains dominating, but rarely governing, likely strengthens their suitability as a source of inspiration rather than weaken it. We are fairly well informed about Galactic Empire's supply of fully operational battle stations in *Star Wars*. We know less about how the Empire handles wage negotiations or pensions.

But identification with dystopia is only one aspect of this now well-established language game among tech companies. The other is disidentification with power. One is a witness to one's own power rather than wielding it. One experiences power as an aesthetic effect in two senses—it doesn't feel entirely real, even when it is deadly real to those upon whom it is exercised. And it is, like sensation in Kant's transcendental aesthetic, something that is given rather than made in its precise parameters. Power is something that happens to the powerful.

DOGE began as a meme, doubly so: The abbreviation for the Department of Government Efficiency is a reference to Musk's favorite meme, which was cool, if ever, about ten years ago. The Doge meme and the associated meme coin became popular in 2013. And the idea that the meme could give Musk's efforts to harrow the federal government their ironic name seems to have started with an AI-generated image that went viral on X in September 2024: It showed a young, square-jawed, broad-shouldered fantasy Musk posing in a leather jacket with sunglasses and a gold chain in front of a "D.O.G.E" plaque. The look was somewhere between rapper, bounty hunter, and Finnish DJ. The logic of disruption is closely allied with the logic of the meme, which rejects established semantic systems and short-circuits them.

It is characteristic of the figure of the college dropout that he maintains a youthful appearance, even if that youth becomes increasingly worn. There is a dynamic of arrested development in people who drop out of college and start companies while still of college age—companies that then strongly resemble a college dorm in their business model, org chart, and corporate culture.

The college dropout is not necessarily a young person, but they always play one on social media. In this context, it seems significant that the memes that Musk and his fans use to illustrate and legitimize their efforts are, by the standards of the social media age, antediluvian. They are flashes in the pan from 2017, when the alt-right was on the rise, 4chan took over right-wing politics, and, as Angela Nagle noted at the time, the memetic energy originated almost exclusively from the right.[11] Just as famous college dropouts à la Mark Zuckerberg left college only to take the logic and habits of college with them everywhere, Musk seems to be dragging the year 2017 with him wherever he goes.

In several interviews, Musk has traced the beginning of his path from "anti-wokeness" to open fascism back to the idea that "the left has banned comedy."[12] I think this persistent self-portrayal suggests two things: First, that journalists and researchers were absolutely right when they said that the kind of meme irony that in 2017 the trolls allegedly only used to scare the normies was in reality just cruelty with a thin veneer of plausible deniability. And second, that this position is profoundly unserious, even where it is absolutely serious in its rhetoric and consequences. In other words: As terrible as it sounds, in his own worldview, Musk cut a grandmother's social security to get a reaction, to trigger others.

One of the questions that has occupied many media outlets in the last three years is: "What happened to Elon Musk?" Well, in a way, nothing at all has happened to him. The idea that established expertise and recognized authority were inherently something deeply illegitimate, even demonic, has always been part of his particular brand of genius aesthetic and contributed to his appeal to the audience for which he performed. Consider the rescue from the Tham Luang cave. In June 2018, twelve members of a youth soccer team and a coach became trapped in an extensive cave system in northern Thailand. The children were trapped in the cave for twelve days while a group of expert cave divers and members of the Thai navy worked to figure out a rescue plan.

To anyone watching the drama, the eventual rescue, which involved thousands of people and cost one Thai Navy diver his life, was a triumph of expertise, expertise that came from quite traditional sources: scientists, a small dedicated community of enthusiasts (in this case, cave divers), Thai bureaucrats, the police and the Thai Navy. Elon Musk experienced something quite different: he planned on building a "kid-sized submarine" to rescue the children, a suggestion Thai authorities and expert divers quickly rejected. Musk immediately understood this rejection as a conspiracy against his genius. He began lashing out at local officials, and infamously asked questions about why a particular British diver should even "be in Thailand," calling him "pedo guy."

This was 2018, the height of QAnon, and accusations of pedophilia were a tried and tested means of casting the normal functioning of institutions in a sinister and conspiratorial light. At the time, few made the connection. Musk's bizarre rants were largely dismissed as part of the billionaire's unpredictability. When seen in the context of QAnon, they were all too predictable. What made them seem so unpredictable was the Silicon Valley aesthetic of genius. Thanks to this aesthetic, an obvious fact became nearly invisible: that here was a rich, aging man following a fairly well-trod path to right-wing radicalization—a path he shared with many at the time, who were much less rich and were not supposed to be geniuses.

Silicon Valley had long cloaked every setback or limitation of its power and influence in a flurry of conspiratorial phrases. Something else is always afoot. Whether it was Peter Thiel's fixation on the play of mimetic desire (in which human desire is entirely a factor of what other people desire); Curtis Yarvin's concept of the "Cathedral" (a cabal of powerful elites that shape the corridor of opinion); or simply Elizabeth Holmes's desperate tap dancing on *Mad Money*: Because of the cult of genius around so many founders, this conspiratorial framing was not usually read as what it was. Is the idea that some ominous "they" prevented the success of some founder's product, that "they" were responsible for every setback from regulators or the public fundamentally different from the kinds of ravings you'd hear about an unfair divorce or a vindictive tax audit from people who've been less lucky in life? The discourse surrounding Silicon Valley's conspiracists had cultivated a sense of distinctness where absolutely none was warranted. Their "they" had to be different, smarter, more profound. Because they were supposedly different, smarter, more profound.

FOUR

Distinction

The personal backgrounds of Silicon Valley's most influential founders display a good deal of uniformity, in terms of both socioeconomics and geography. Another point of commonality has to do with history: the founders may not be part of a generation narrowly defined, but they share a historically specific frame of cultural reference. Silicon Valley has long been dominated by certain age cohorts. Indeed, the success of individual companies (and of the ecosystem as a whole) surely has something to do with the fact that its networks tend to connect people of very similar age. The money man, the founder who pitches him, the rank-and-file coders and the in-house counsel of a young company frequently are on the same wavelength because they have the exact same background, have grown up with the same cultural codes, or have even slurped instant ramen in the same dorms. Of course, they will rarely see it this way themselves.

The "traitorous eight" may not all have attended the same college, but they were in the same age cohort. When William Shockley recruited the eight young men in 1956 for Shockley Semiconductor Laboratories, the first company on the San Francisco peninsula to work on silicon-based chips, they were all recent college graduates, all born between 1922 and 1927. Shockley, who had worked at Bell Labs and had done research for the armed forces during the war, was a Nobel laureate, but also an authoritarian, paranoid boss, who seemed to expect the kinds of hierarchical structure that still dominated business and the military in the 1950s. The eight young engineers almost immediately took exception to Shockley's leadership style and defected from the company in what must count as record time.[1] By 1957 the company had lost its leadership team, Shockley was publicly humiliated, and Shockley Semiconductors was more or less over. The birth of Silicon Valley was thus a moment of an ur-horde of sons killing their father figure. Or, better put, it was oedipal in a strange way, which has since become characteristic for Silicon Valley. The young rebelled against the old, freed themselves—only to then pretty much continue doing what the old had been doing all along. Shockley's sorcerer's apprentices continued Shockley's works, with the same pitch and the same money, just without Shockley.[2]

Julius Blank, Victor Grinich, Jean Hoerni, Eugene Kleiner, Jay Last, Gordon Moore, Robert Noyce, and Sheldon Roberts founded a new company, Fairchild Semiconductor, from which over time several other microchip companies spun off. Among the "Fairchildren" were Intel and AMD, but so were venture companies like Kleiner Perkins. Like the "PayPal Mafia" of the late 1990s, the "traitorous eight" were fairly homogeneous in their backgrounds, their age profiles, and their management styles. And they were the grandfathers of today's Silicon Valley. The VCs who funded their endeavors were very similar people: investor and inventor spoke the same language, specifically because they shared the same generational experience.

When compared to the "traitorous eight" or even the PayPal Mafia, the generation of founders and their backers that have dominated headlines and the contemporary image of Silicon Valley appears a bit more diffuse. Still, the age cohort remains a clearly identifiable phenomenon in the Valley, in particular since so many cofounders met in college. Steve Jobs and Bill Gates are the same age; Sergey Brin and Larry Page, who met at Stanford, were both born in 1973. Mark Zuckerberg and the entire original inner circle of Facebook were the same age, which is the same age as Instagram's founders Kevin Systrom and Mike Krieger. It's not really true, as is sometimes said, that through tech our world is dominated by solitary geniuses. It is dominated by cliques of people who are more or less the same age.

If they're basically part of the same generation, what was the nature of their generational experience? With some exceptions, they were children of privileged, middle-class households, usually highly credentialed members of what Barbara and John Ehrenreich called the "professional-managerial class."[3] Page and Brin are children of college professors (Michigan State and University of Maryland, respectively); Zuckerberg is the son of a dentist and a psychiatrist;

Evan Spiegel is the child of two lawyers. Kevin Systrom's parents worked at a dot-com. These men definitely climbed the social ladder, but they did so from affluence to megawealth, from golf course or country club to the superyacht club.

After World War II, the United States experienced a great deal of upward social mobility, driven by the expansion of the education sector through government subsidies and due to the unequal distribution of its windfalls enforced by racial segregation. It seems important that neither these young men nor their families were part of this uplift. Rather, their families tended to be in the professions that earn money by managing the uplift of others. I don't know anything about the political outlook of any of their families. But it seems interesting that for families such as theirs, upward mobility represented both their raison d'être and a possible threat. After all, it was their job to create and groom the potential competition. Or—more to the point—their sons' potential competition.

Part of these founders' patrimony is not depending on things other people depend on. Another part is the fear of falling that emerges when part of your job is to create more people like yourself. As more Americans entered the middle class, dentists, lawyers, professors, and programmers were forced to ask themselves how to stand out from the new arrivals. Their sons, the generation of founders, had a different but related problem: How to distinguish yourself amid a mass of very similar-looking young people of very similar backgrounds.

That experience has left its mark on their pitches, whether they bring the pitches to potential funders or whether they are the ones funding them. The fact that other people coming up in the world matters to them, but mostly because it legitimates their own position. "This university will lift you into the middle class" has turned into "my platform will lift some people into the middle class." But that uplift also constitutes a threat: if the mechanism were to work too well, your own position might be in danger. Doing your job well means you create your own competition, water down your own uniqueness. This probably explains a peculiarity of the companies created by this generation: they present themselves as born levelers, democratizers, equalizers. And yet they seem to operate with the harshest of hierarchies.

Drivers for Uber and Lyft do not have a seat at the sushi bar amid the programmers at the company headquarters who make the real money. And Meta or Google's campuses have intricate geographies of caste, with various badges giving you access to a very different menu of perks, most of which are completely inaccessible to the armies of junior-level coders and systems analysts who work for various subcontractors. These companies like to demonstratively link arms with a vast army of users, and yet they are surprisingly keen to draw tight boundaries around their own company. Silicon Valley has a mania for distinction: which badge you have decides whether you can take the shuttle or eat the free burrito. Yes, it can tell you who is a "real" employee, and who is whatever the opposite of a real employee is. Massification and distinction are the contradictory basic impulses in this industry. And that contradiction is a reflection of the founders.

In every biography of a famous Silicon Valley founder, you encounter this fear of the masses. Young men like them—upper-middle-class boys who had a thing for computers—were a dime a dozen in the 1990s and aughts. That is their basic trauma. It is a fact they cannot and will not face. The question of how to distinguish yourself from cohort-mates that are, when you're honest, more or less identical to you, is their big question. And they are addicted to stories that allow them to duck that question, that give them a sense of specialness and distinctness.

But the fear of being like others doesn't just shape the individual origin stories but also the institutions created by Silicon Valley founders. Not only its most successful entrepreneurs, but really the entire industry is deeply allergic to imitation. Which is all the stranger because they're constantly busy imitating each other. Going to a party in the Valley long meant pretending an app that was basically Uber for lawnmowers was the height of originality and genius.

The investor and billionaire Peter Thiel is obsessed with the idea that all desire is mimetic, and that this makes humanity eminently predictable. Humanity? Well, certain people—what am I saying, certain geniuses—who have cracked the code of mimetic desire can rise above the level of mere mortals and can direct and manipulate the herd. Granted, that's a pretty antidemocratic way of thinking. More interesting, perhaps, is its psychological dimension. Recall how Peter Thiel made his money. He helped found PayPal, a payment system so similar to X.com (not the one you're thinking of, but also run by Elon Musk) and BillPoint that eBay bought all three and integrated them. He then became even richer with a MySpace clone called Facebook, which ended up beating out a handful of more or less identical competitors. Mimesis may be Thiel's greatest fear. He also seems to owe his fortune to it.

In a system of repetition and highly limited variation, the fear of being overtaken is going to be particularly acute. A few years ago I spoke with Martin Pichinson, an LA-based attorney who over the years has carved out for himself a peculiar niche in the Silicon Valley life cycle. He buries failed start-ups. Pichinson told me that most of his unfortunate clients were not felled by bad ideas or incompetence; many, he told me, were brilliant. They simply hadn't been first.[4]

Sometime in the 2010s, I met with a former student who had left the university to join a start-up founded by other Stanford students. The company had started its seed round with enormous plaudits. Marc Andreessen, Peter Thiel, and Richard Branson had invested. The company had made an impressive ad. And then it had gone sort of quiet. When I asked my former student about this, he was happy to explain their pitch. I asked innocently what set them apart from a new service that one of the big tech companies was starting to introduce on their devices. He gave me a sheepish grin and went on explaining. So it's like the new Apple product, I said, and immediately regretted my comment. He looked physically pained. I am pretty sure that the start-up was, at this point, already a zombie. Everyone knew that it had had a real shot, and that it had missed its window. But the seed money wasn't used up, so the company persisted, a boat against the current. What really made an impression on me was that this trajectory seemed to cause my student—who was, after all, entirely guiltless in the matter—immense anguish. Coming in second caused him physical discomfort.

All their lives these young men have been told how special they are, all ample evidence to the contrary notwithstanding. Decades ago, telling them how special they are was a job for their college classes, IQ tests, comics, or science fiction books. Today it is ours, with cover stories, endless interviews, and, well, books about how these men think and govern. Because these young men grew up among the accreditors, they like praise that transcends traditional accreditation. As kids, they were in various gifted programs; today, some suck-up on X calls them a genius.

Historian Quinn Slobodian points out that in Silicon Valley, more so than elsewhere, neoliberalism went along with a broad range of pseudoscience.[5] Today, that pseudoscience is billionaires trying to beat the aging process, as in the case of venture capitalist Bryan Johnson, or vaccine denialism, as in the case of Nicole Shanahan (ex-wife of Sergey Brin and former vice presidential running mate to RFK Jr.). And it's always been eugenics. But this sustained interest in pseudoscience is more than a mere eccentricity, or a sign that Silicon Valley billionaires may have more power than good sense. Rather, this interest articulates a political position, one that is essential to Silicon Valley's power and influence.

As Slobodian argues, starting in the 1990s, neoliberalism found a new point of orientation: nature. This reorientation had two results: on the one hand a belief in the "naturalness" of certain hierarchies, and on the other a distrust of state interventions that treated these hierarchies as man-made and sought to attenuate them. By making a fetish of supposedly natural givens, this kind of thinking could present itself as libertarian, while sounding surprisingly traditionalist.

In 1996, President Bill Clinton signed the Telecommunications Act—a joint project between a Democratic president and a very conservative Republican Congress. As the media scholar Becca Lewis has noted, those conservatives and traditionalists who had come to power with Newt Gingrich's "Contract for America" had good reason to vote for the Telecommunications Act.[6] For one, because the act focused on pornography and "inappropriate material" on the internet. But for another, because it combined the values of conservatism via its censorship provisions with clearly libertarian premises. At a 1994 panel, the libertarian Progress and Freedom Foundation (PFF) promised that the internet would yield "a future like *The Jetsons* with the values of *The Little House on the Prairie*," "the 2040s and the 1840s coming together." The way Washington viewed Silicon Valley was long dominated by this particular wish, to see future and tradition united in one.[7]

According to PFF, the internet would make it easier to get women to stay home (or at least to work from home). And it would weaken the state: the PFF popularized a new metaphor as a counterpoint of the "data superhighway"—namely, "cyberspace." A space, in other words, that individuals and families would be able to settle and colonize. What the internet was never allowed to be, and what it did not become, not least of all after the Telecommunications Act of 1996: a government project. "Cyberspace: It's Nobody's Highway," as a PFF slogan would have it. Meaning: it was space to be colonized by individual settlers in neat family units, not to be made accessible through government investment and regulation. And George Gilder, a 1970s antifeminist gadfly who reinvented himself as a prophet of Silicon Valley in the 1980s, described the tech entrepreneur as essentially an artistic genius: "Because they can change the technical frontiers and reshape public desires, entrepreneurs may be even less limited by tastes and technologies than artists and writers, who are widely seen as supremely free."[8]

So far, so triumphalist. But dominance had an odd role to play in this discourse. As a desideratum it is paramount. But in fact it never becomes quite real. The dominance tech entrepreneurship *should* by rights have attained is forever frustrated—by an interventionist state, by civil rights, by the leveling tendencies of democracy. Which is why this discourse manages the feat of being structurally conservative and revolutionary at once. Because the whole language game depends on the idea that the "wrong" kind of people are dominant everywhere. This idea has a long and curious tradition in Silicon Valley. The fact that the Valley as a region has long managed to be both dominant and marginal may have helped keep that tradition alive there.

The botanist, eugenicist, and peace activist David Starr Jordan wrote in 1903 that the Civil War had delivered "the best" of the "race" unto death; those Americans who took their place and sired the youth of his own day, he thought genetically inferior. The wrong kinds of Americans predominated in 1903, because the right kinds of Americans had been needlessly sacrificed between 1861 and 1865. When he wrote his pamphlet, Jordan was president of Stanford, the university's first. In 1965 a Stanford professor gave a long interview to *U.S. News & World Report* with a similar thesis. In the United States, he claimed, the "abundant welfare state" all but insured that unfit and less intelligent people "will be multiplying at an enormously faster rate than more intelligent people do."[9] That professor was none other than William Shockley, who had begun teaching at the university after his company failed. And who had turned his yen for hierarchies into speculations about race, the welfare state, and intelligence.

This argument attained its modern form in Charles Murray and Richard Herrnstein's *The Bell Curve*, which was published in 1994. The two made the same argument as Shockley before them—that the welfare state subsidized "births among poor women . . . who are disproportionately at the lower end of the intelligence distribution"—but this time under the banner of "group IQ."[10] According to Quinn Slobodian, this marked the comeback of the IQ concept among American conservatives. And even during times when Silicon Valley presented itself as far more liberal than it does today, it could still be enthusiastic about IQ.

One reason for this may be that the myth of masses of intellectually inferior people threatening to overwhelm the "high-IQ individuals" served as a kind of antidote to the biographical anxieties and generational self-doubt of many technologists. Granted, there were young, male programmers everywhere you looked. Thanks to the IQ discourse, however, they were still a finite, precious resource. "We have to treat our high-IQ people well," Donald Trump warned in the spring of 2025. "Because we don't have many of them." He was standing next to Elon Musk at the time. And just in case the eugenic implications weren't clear enough, it's worth looking at the people Trump has criticized as "low-IQ individuals"—they are almost without exception Black or Latino, and often also women.

Indeed, the past thirty years have seen the emergence of a specific type of discourse participant: the IQ nerd. Especially in the United States, there is a specific type of man (and it is almost always a man) who knows his IQ precisely, considers his own IQ extremely important, and frequently mentions it. Above all, however, the IQ nerd operates with it as a familiar and unproblematic quantity: He can use it to explain politics, the demographic homogeneity of his circle of friends, and—above all—his dating experiences.

This does not mean the IQ nerd places great emphasis on intelligence, education, or similar qualities. No, the IQ nerd uses IQ almost in isolation, sometimes in opposition to everything else. When such people talk about "IQ," it's no longer an interpretation of reality but a language game that is only interested in very specific questions, future scenarios, and cultural phenomena. Slobodian, therefore, also speaks of IQ fetishism: talking about and focusing on IQ reduces relationships between people—sometimes very complex ones—to an easily manageable number. A number to which one can cling and in which one can take refuge.

Many of the tech moguls are IQ nerds, and they surround themselves with similar people: at the beginning of 2025, dozens of journalists and public intellectuals in the United States engaged in a vigorous debate about how high Elon Musk's IQ might be. His IQ was, as journalist Amanda Hess wrote, "extrapolated from his success, his wealth, his biography, and his personal presentation."[11]

Today, the wealthy of Silicon Valley are implementing the eugenics projects of previous generations. From Elon Musk's dozens of DNA-screened children to the countless genetic testing start-ups offering their services in the Valley, many in the new tech elite see genetic predisposition as a corrective to what they perceive as a hopelessly corrupt and corrupting state with its democratic rights for all and its equalizing educational institutions. Charles Murray, too, admires Musk for his IQ and sees him as "the legitimate heir of George Mueller, Wernher von Braun, and George Low." Except that he has to work in the private sector and not at NASA. Why? Today's NASA is "preoccupied with checking off its DEI boxes."[12] By "DEI"—diversity, equity, and inclusion—American conservatives mean all efforts within American society to promote diversity, and increasingly, simply the presence of nonwhite or nonmale people in positions of authority and esteem. For people like Murray, a company like Musk's SpaceX has always represented two things: a triumph of the free market over the state, and a triumph of white men over a pluralistic society.

Whether in the discourse on AI, on "DEI," or on IQ: On the one hand, Silicon Valley elites believe that leadership is in their blood. On the other hand, it clearly isn't. Theirs is a form of dominance that doesn't quite believe in itself. Anyone who observes the alpha males of Silicon Valley quickly encounters the thin-skinned nature and extreme insecurity of these figures. Their companies emulate their founders, managing to see themselves as underdogs even amid their absolute dominance. This is as true of Peter Thiel as an individual, who seems to understand the CEO as a sacrificial lamb à la Jesus, as it is of the defensive posture that even the largest corporations in Silicon Valley instinctively adopt at the slightest hint of criticism. It's certainly partly rhetoric, but when someone so frequently and reflexively resorts to this kind of thinking, the idea is clearly ingrained. These men have an extremely keen sense of who deserves power. And according to their own way of stratifying the world, they are unsure whether they deserve it themselves.

In 1942, the philosopher Alexandre Kojève wrote a short text titled "The Notion of Authority."[13] For Kojève, all authority presupposed "the possibility of opposing it" and the "voluntary renunciation of that possibility."[14] Authority possesses legitimacy in the eyes of those who exercise it and in the eyes of those who submit to it. As soon as it takes on a character of inevitability and others accommodate themselves to it without accepting it as legitimate, it is no longer authority. This description of "authority," honed on the experience of Vichy France, reflects the form of dominance that Silicon Valley companies have gained in our world over the past twenty years: people acquiesce to its inevitability, but they hardly affirm it. And strangely enough, the companies themselves seem to see it this way themselves: If they don't do it, someone else will.

Kojève goes on: "By exercising authority, the agent can change the outward human given without suffering a repercussion from the action, i.e., without himself changing as a result of his action."[15] We don't resent genuine authority for having to submit to it. It neither loses nor gains legitimacy in its application. Two things stand out with regard to Silicon Valley's dominance. First, it is of a completely different nature. The application of dominance and its legitimacy seem to be in an inverse relationship: the more you capitulate to it, the more it annoys you. And second, the idea of an authority that can act "without suffering a repercussion" clearly stands as an unattainable ideal behind Silicon Valley's mindset of dominance. This is how they would like it to be, and the fury of an Elon Musk, a Mark Zuckerberg, a Marc Andreessen is that of the disappointed romantic who cannot see in the mirror the image he has of himself.

Years ago, I would have had to consult a psychoanalyst in San Francisco or Mountain View to find out what image these men have of themselves. Today I no longer need to, because they will tweet this image out with some regularity: AI-generated slop, that is, massively and uniformly generated AI images, showing the CEOs, politicians, and right-wing influencers in all sorts of heroic poses and costumes, and which, especially by Elon Musk, are eagerly shared with followers. Musk loves depictions of himself—always with that chin and the hair he either wishes he had or that he thinks he has—as a Roman centurion, a soldier, or a Space Marine from the Warhammer 40,000 miniature game. He doesn't usually create them himself; instead, fans or other users ask Dall-E or similar services: "Show me a picture of Elon Musk as a soldier in World War II." And then they share the resulting fascist kitsch on X, hoping that Musk will repost it and they can earn a few hundred dollars.

As art historian Roland Meyer has shown, the historical costume is always a sham: the AI jumbles signifiers together and generates the idea of "Rome" rather than a genuine historical costume. This is precisely what Musk seems to like: his hagiography thrives on associations that arise almost randomly from probabilistic data. It is an image of power that doesn't need to affirmatively refer to actually existing power, either in the past or the present. The far-right ideology from which this springs is recognizable primarily by the semantic fields—in other words, the associations that the user incorporated into their prompt. At the same time, the arbitrariness of the AI aesthetic naturally undermines the sense of power that the image is meant to embody for someone like Musk. Certainly, he has enough fans who are willing to create such images for him. But he must also be aware that these same fans might, in the next breath, ask Dall-E for "fake porn of Jenna Ortega" or "giraffes with enormous breasts." Even in the moment of his heroization, this man is being processed through the same digital sausage grinder as cat pictures or hentai pornography.[16]

Silicon Valley's companies haven't seized power; they've seized the simulation of power. A simulation that doesn't even believe in itself. This makes them susceptible to modern populism, which doesn't believe in its own populism, and to authoritarianism, which never truly considers itself in power, not even when it exercises power dictatorially. With our police who never claim to be in control of the situation, our elites who consider themselves anti-elite, while deeming trans people and high school teachers part of the elite. Silicon Valley is a driving force behind the characteristic self-deceptions of our time. But on a more banal level, it simply tells itself the same lies as everyone else. The inability of the powerful to understand or grasp the extent and essence of their power has profound consequences for the politics of this historical moment. Not least because the same inability exists among many of the elites in business and the media.

In 1992, George Gilder wrote a new edition of his book on the genius of capitalism. The first version from 1984 was still entirely focused on semiconductors. In 1992, however, software naturally dominated, and above all, Bill Gates. What hadn't changed was Gilder's veneration of the unique, world-shattering entrepreneur (he didn't seem to notice any female entrepreneurs). These men, he wrote, "didn't climb hierarchies, they created new ones. . . . They didn't climb to the top, they made themselves the top."[17]

In Gilder's enthusiastic praise, two things stand out: the cult of disruption and something far more sinister, the cult of personality. The veneration of CEOs has long served as a cover for an authoritarian streak in US politics. This is even more evident in other countries, such as Germany and Switzerland, where the fascination with tech CEOs has become a means of embracing authoritarianism without having to admit it to others or to oneself. Experts gleefully celebrate when the Mandarin class is overthrown and dusty democratic norms are shattered—and, should there be any backlash, they can still claim they are only talking about economics, even though they are actually talking about democratic governance.

The idea that the government should be run like a business is a trope in American political discourse, so much so that its distinctly authoritarian implications are often overlooked. Sociologists warn that obedience to the "economy" can carry the seed of a "secondary authoritarianism" in which individuals are expected not to submit to the will of the nation but to sacrifice themselves on the altar of the "economy." This economy, as sociologist Oliver Decker points out, is strangely and profoundly inscrutable—it is a god that reflects back to its soothsayers whatever they want to find in it. Yet, its demand remains equally unremitting.[18]

But the demands of "the economy" were, in a way, the euphemistic arsenal of the 1990s and early aughts. Today, remarkably, we are being asked to make similar sacrifices, but on the altar of innovation, specifically the innovation embodied by the whims of a few geniuses. In other words, it mostly goes unmentioned that this is ultimately a way of pushing the dissonances of pluralism into the background in favor of the more powerful aesthetic of the leadership principle. The brilliant CEO is (a) an avatar of what "the market" or "the future" wants from us, the world spirit not quite on horseback, but on a wakeboard. The brilliant CEO is also (b) a decidedly creaturely being, whose food intake, daily habits, hobbies, and quirks are analyzed by both the court press and subordinates. Nobody cared what kind of juice the financier Jerome Kohlberg or auto industry icon Lee Iacocca drank. Nobody cared about Samuel Goldwyn's mindfulness practice.

The tech genius as a figure is a version of what Ernst Kantorowicz described as the King's Two Bodies:[19] the bearer of a metaphysical essence, albeit hailing not from a dynastic past but from a promised future, and a spectacularly fallible being. It's no coincidence that Peter Thiel seems to view the CEO as Jesus—a sacrificial lamb whose flesh is always ready to be mortified. Or whose creaturely preoccupations at their most bizarre are exposed when, for example, he publishes his speculations that CEOs are like Jesus on a platform that he doesn't fully own.

Let me briefly return to the Tham Luang cave. You might be wondering: Why? It's such a small and embarrassing episode. But consider that the media probably didn't draw any conclusions from the cave incident and the endless parade of similar Musk fiascos because it was so minor, because it was so embarrassing. And because it was difficult to feature a billionaire on the cover as a savior, visionary, and genius who could explain where the world, civilization, humanity were headed. Only to then, on page three, have him talking about cave divers being sex tourists.

One only has to look at the kind of fawning coverage that Silicon Valley billionaires have enjoyed in recent years. Consider Michael Lewis's *Going Infinite*, a book about the crypto entrepreneur and convicted fraudster Sam Bankman-

Fried. The author desperately tries to convince his reader—and, it seems, ultimately himself—that mundane details in Bankman-Fried's biography indicate that "SBF" is in fact an absolute genius: "During lectures, he had felt a boredom that amounted to physical pain. He couldn't stand pre-packaged chatter. He always knew in advance what the professor was getting at with what he was saying, and bang, he could no longer concentrate."[20]

A freshman who gets bored during a lecture? A college student who thinks he already knows what the professor is getting at? Groundbreaking. Sam Bankman-Fried seems to have told author Lewis a set of fairly ordinary stories, the types of stories you would hear from any person like Sam Bankman-Fried. And Lewis dutifully spun them into tales of solitary genius. The result is a boomerang of vicarious embarrassment: a story like this makes both SBF and his biographer look like fools. Silicon Valley's young entrepreneurs—or at least those who become famous—are often so open about their neediness and complexes that we are drawn to them and repelled at the same time. They make us complicit in their most embarrassing foibles. By observing them, one becomes a courtier in Hans Christian Andersen's fairy tale.

Crucially, however, without the income of a courtier. Many successful CEOs in Silicon Valley have perfected personal neediness and interpersonal deficits into just another form of labor extraction. This is precisely the form behind the attention we are forced to give today to the most absurd and bizarre antics of billionaires. Let's return to the image of Elon Musk with which DOGE's ominous crash through the institutions began. It's worth considering the path this image took from its creator—whoever that may have been. It's unlikely that Musk created it himself; he is notorious for stealing memes, and that seems to be the most likely theory here.

On X, there are countless Musk memes on offer. Whoever created the original DOGE meme showing Elon Musk with the "Department of Government Efficiency" sign, it's unlikely they hoped Musk would steal it. The creator of the image probably hoped for the kind of treatment that other flattering AI images of Musk receive from the subject: a retweet or a reply from Musk. That's why Musk slop invariably presents the billionaire the way he probably wishes he looked. Hence the reference to Musk's favorite meme, "DOGE."

Users who engage with Musk in this way are vying for more than just attention or approval. The vast majority of them has a small blue checkmark next to their name, meaning they can convert the attention they receive on X into money. Previously, the blue checkmark was an indicator of established authorities (such as CNN or the *Washington Post*) or well-known people (celebrities, journalists, politicians). Today, it primarily means: people who like Elon and know how to capitalize on it. The resulting financial system is somewhat bizarre. For blue-check users in particular, a reply to or repost of Musk's content to his over two hundred million followers on his platform, where he regularly amplifies his own content and suppresses that of others, is literally worth money. The younger generation calls what these users are doing "catfishing": they create portraits (always flattering, always beautifying, always rejuvenating) to entice the platform's ruler into sharing their content. They appeal to his deepest vanity. But given the neofeudal nature of their relationship, there's no guarantee that his attention will actually translate into broader recognition or financial gain. Because, as the anonymous creator of the DOGE image learned, Musk can simply steal their image, and they get nothing. More and more people have become sycophants to the narcissism of our tech elite, and it's striking that money is becoming increasingly incidental and irrelevant in this dynamic. The real currency is distinctness.

FIVE

Maturity

In October 2022, Elon Musk walked through the glass doors of Twitter's Market Street headquarters in San Francisco. The billionaire, who was about to acquire the social network, had not arrived empty-handed. He had brought a sink with him and soon shared a short video clip of himself carrying said sink into the modern lobby. "Let that sink in." The play on words was a hit with a very specific group of internet users—people who were drawn to a certain brand of meme humor that had perhaps seen better days. And who now got to celebrate the fact that one of their own was taking over the messaging service that had been frying their brains—and his.

Who exactly took over Twitter that day? Sure, the man with the sink was the new owner. But he was also, to some extent, simply a Twitter fan, one of many. Someone who spent a lot of time, perhaps too much time, on the network. Perhaps he was even something of a Twitter victim. Not only had his political pronouncements over the previous five years closely resembled what your Facebook- or Twitter-poisoned uncle posts in the family chat, only to be studiously ignored by the rest of the family. Even Musk's purchase had begun as a joke, in the back-and-forth sallies of quote-tweets and replies. Once Musk realized what he had done, he tried to back out of the deal. And like a man who clicks on a Twitter link to buy an exercise machine and only later reads the reviews, Elon Musk eventually decided to settle into the world his humiliation created.

At least, that's how it appeared to many media outlets, to many in Silicon Valley, to many who (still) worked at Twitter. But Musk also has a fan base. And the stupid stunt with the sink was for them. Exactly who was the target audience for this performance? As so often, Musk's instincts ran toward a rather dated brand of meme humor. When the old guard at Fox News comment "very funny," as they dutifully did, you know the joker isn't exactly on the cutting edge of comedy. Immediately after the bit with the sink, Musk issued a statement: "The reason I bought Twitter is because it is important for the future of civilization to have a common digital town square."[1] A few days later, he posted a picture of a mattress on which the "Chief Twit," then fifty-two years old, was allegedly sleeping at work.

Let's assume you'd never heard of Elon Musk or Twitter and were presented with these scenes out of context: How old would you imagine this person to be? The answer is probably: You can't say, he's almost every age at once. The desperate pandering meme humor for a pack of online cheerleaders make him sound like a teenager. But then again, the stale memes and dad jokes sound more like a longtime gamer who's now in their mid-thirties. The mattress in the office feels like it comes from the kit of a twenty-two-year-old Stanford dropout. The statement about the "future of civilization"? From a mature, middle-aged thinker. The reception on Fox News? Would put him safely in the silver hair brigade.

There was a historic moment when the young men of Silicon Valley colonized the imagination of the entire world. It was a moment when the world—or a part of it—got to, or longed to, recognize itself in them. More precisely, recognize itself in their youth. Their youth gave the sluggishness and exhaustion of capitalism, the tedium of long-established privileges and hierarchies a fresh coat of paint. But youth has a way of fading, and a fresh coat of paint has a way of peeling off. The process of disillusionment with figures like Musk and Zuckerberg is one with their aging process.

So what happens when these professional young people grow old? What happens to a youth that is supposed to stand in for our youth, the youth of capitalism, the youth of the West, the youth of the established elite? When the large corporations that now dominate the perception of Silicon Valley were still in their infancy, the youth of the inventors guaranteed that the companies they led still had a runway. There was still enough world and time to eventually fulfill their promises—even if the road to profitability involved turning right at the second star and going straight on 'til morning. Through their promises of deliverables, of profitability, of technological solutions to social problems, their unwritten future was also ours.

But nothing is less uplifting than having a great future behind you. And because both traditional media and the social media platforms they created obsessively focus the public's attention on the founders, we are now witnesses to a far less uplifting spectacle: their undignified aging process. Whether it's Elon Musk's X or Mark Zuckerberg's empty "metaverse": the user of yesteryear has mutated, been demoted. On Facebook, we, or at least our attention, were still currency. On Twitter "our eyeballs" is how the company hoped to eventually become profitable. The Metaverse and X are no longer profit-driven; they operate on a different principle. They have no choice but to function, and not because the fabulously wealthy owners wouldn't otherwise make money. They're probably losing money. No, they continue to exist entirely to flatter, or else protect, the owners' narcissism.

In late summer 2024, two years after Elon Musk's acquisition of Twitter, the company's advertising revenue had plummeted by roughly half. This also meant that the service was generating less in advertising revenue than Elon Musk had to pay in interest on the loans he had taken out to buy it. Many former advertisers had decided to stop buying spots on a website that barely moderated its content, that many former users were abandoning, and that frequently crashed completely. So Musk decided to sue these departing advertisers, forcing them to advertise with him.[2]

Musk's acquisition of Twitter has, in many ways, exposed for a sham the voluntarism that had so long defined Silicon Valley's pitch. The old argument was: Why would you want to ruin these platforms—through regulation, for instance—for the people who flock to them in the millions? But in Musk's lawsuits, we observe the opposite: a world in which we supposedly owe our patronage, our attention, to the right-wing power users and the equally right-wing extremist CEO of a platform. Some users leave or avoid these platforms because they are disappointed by the founders or the platform itself. Many users, however, leave because they simply don't know what the platform still needs them for. Twitter's reactionaries have a perfect term for a person who's simply sort of there, and whose function it is to watch helplessly: a cuck. Musk's purchase of Twitter was a bid to turn millions of users into cucks.

At the same time, however, Silicon Valley's products have absolutized lack of dignity—not just that of the CEOs who do their most embarrassing aging in plain view, but for just about everyone who uses their services. Thanks to social media, our aging processes, our declining mental acuity desperately clinging to anecdotes, phrases, images, have become a spectacle for other, younger generations. There are now only two types of users: those who have made their home in a parallel world of AI garbage, phishing spam, and fake news, to the gleeful delight of younger generations. And those who will suffer that fate in a few years or decades. In the age of social media, we are maturing backward. The platform has a never-ending runway. All the problems—the Nazis, the spam, the bots, the fake news—are simply signs that the product is still maturing.

And what about those of us who use these platforms? For us, the same "runway" is constantly shrinking: With every click, with every "like" under an obviously AI-generated image, with every breathless forward to exasperated younger family members, we tick toward the only singularity in life that is unavoidable. The point at which we are as dead as Twitter.

In his *Elements of the Philosophy of Right*, Hegel describes a system of "estates." In modern societies, individuals have different ways of relating their needs, means, and contributions to the common good. These different ways taken together determine their membership in an "estate." For Hegel, "determining" always means picking out something particular from the universal, while other possibilities are ruled out. Belonging to an estate is thus the same thing as saying: I contribute to the "system of needs" through *x* and *y*, but not through *z*. "The individual attains actuality only by entering . . . into determinate particularity; he must accordingly limit himself exclusively to one of the particular spheres of need."[3]

Behind what Hegel, in a somewhat old-fashioned turn of phrase, calls "honor of one's estate," there hovers an extremely modern question: how do individual people become "a member of one of the moments of civil society"[4] and how do they get recognized as such by themselves and "in the eyes of others"? Again, Hegel thinks that this recognition has an inclusive and an exclusive element: we are recognized as being *x* and *y*, but not *z*. Part of being in society is selecting things for which we wish to be recognized, and that—tragically, inescapably—also means consenting to not being recognized for other things. Hegel then sketches a negative type, one who eludes this "honor of one's estate." Someone who chooses not to choose. Hegel acknowledges that it is understandable that "initially—i.e. especially in youth—the individual balks at the notion of committing himself to a particular estate, and regards this as a limitation imposed on his universal determination and as a purely external necessity." This, the philosopher claims, is a fallacy, purely "abstract" thinking.[5]

The person Hegel describes thinks any particular "estate" would unduly restrict them and prefers to remain undetermined. It is easy to detect in Hegel's brief description of this perpetual youth the irritation of old age, which emphasizes that growing older inevitably means closing certain doors and assuming certain liabilities. However, this is not exactly what Hegel is saying—at least not if we consider Hegel's project in the *Elements* as a whole. Hegel's intention in the book is to develop the essence of human freedom. His point, therefore, is not that it is immature not to choose a station in life. Rather, he thinks that it is unfree.

His argument goes as follows: Logically speaking, freedom cannot consist of simply doing what we want. For what we want depends on chance and circumstance, on our appetites and whims, and these are, as is well known, not usually compatible with autonomy. No, freedom consists rather in determining ourselves. We obey a law, but one we have given ourselves. The opposite, when the subject does whatever springs to its mind, Hegel calls arbitrariness. And because it cannot give any reasons for doing what it is doing at any given moment, except that it just happened to occur to it ("contingency in the shape of will"[6]), the subject directed by arbitrariness is not free.

In the case of the perpetual adolescent who refuses to commit to a social role, Hegel is therefore not saying: This person is immature. He wants to say: This person is fully determined by things outside of their own person. They cannot decide how they present themselves to others, how they want to be taken seriously, how they want to be recognized and judged, and how they do not. This is a subject whose sheer abundance of designs prevents them from becoming something they can explain to others (or even to themselves).

I think this portrait describes a man like Elon Musk all too well. He wants to be everything at once: a deep thinker and a nihilistic shitposter, a world-saving messiah and a crude cynic, a James Bond villain and a visionary rebel, a comedian and a politician. And in all of this, he seems—like the person Hegel describes—driven, rather than in charge. He desperately wants to be funny, collects comedians, steals their material, and tries to appear on their shows. He wants to be the chill dude smoking a joint on Joe Rogan's podcast. The far-sighted thinker, the otherworldly inventor, the noble defender of our world and values. And the monkish workaholic who sleeps at work and lives only for the product.

He wants to be recognized as a computer gamer. Musk told Joe Rogan he was among the "top 20 players worldwide" playing Blizzard Interactive's Diablo IV. He also appeared to be among the best in Path of Exile 2. The video game community long viewed these claims skeptically: As *The Guardian* wrote, the billionaire "would need to have played hundreds of hours in between running businesses including Tesla Inc, X and SpaceX, as well as his growing political activity alongside Donald Trump."[7] Musk eventually had to admit that he had paid others to grind video games for him.

The anecdote is almost a little touching. The utter joylessness of paying someone to do something for you that's supposed to be fun and relaxing, just so you, the richest man in the world, can get a few online gamers to admire you, feels both pathetic and tragic. More importantly, Musk seems to have envisioned two parallel lives that no amount of world and time would allow to coexist: that of the gamer who wastes endless hours trying to master Diablo IV, and that of the entrepreneur who spends the same amount of time getting richer. He saw both lives and wanted to live them simultaneously. And he fails because of one of the tragic constants of human life: that you only live it once, that every decision contributes to who you are—but also to who you aren't.

Getting to live several lives at once is a utopian idea, but in Musk life it's distorted into caricature. It would be so wonderful to be able to live two, three, or even infinitely many lives side by side or one after the other. We all know that small, entirely private piece of utopia: keeping doors open that, in the "normal" course of one's biography—what literary scholar Elizabeth Freeman has termed "chrononormativity"[8]—would have closed long ago. When I was young there were still men my grandfather's age with gigantic model train sets in their basement. The childlike joy with which these old men bent over this hobby that had preserved youth into old age, seemed for them to represent a temporary rejection of the logic of maturation and age.

But Musk's life isn't utopian. On the one hand, the simultaneity of mutually exclusive elements in his life doesn't run on anything as pure as joy, it is simply a coefficient of seigneurial privilege. He's allowed to do it; the rest of humanity isn't. On the other hand, every one of the roles Musk slips into comes with its own system of obligations and dependencies. He wants to be a hardcore gamer? Fine, but then he shouldn't cheat. He wants to be a comedian?

Then he should work on his material. He wants to be a thinker? Well, then he should think. Musk takes no responsibility for the lives he inhabits. In his anthropology, Immanuel Kant described "that property of the will according to which the subject binds itself to certain practical principles which it has irrevocably prescribed for itself by its own reason" as character.[9] What Musk has chosen as a system is a systematic, and unfortunately widespread, form of characterlessness.

In that sense, Musk's enthusiasm for AI-generated images of himself is another triumph of the imaginary over the grim reality, which is this: Elon Musk is not a warrior of some galactic empire, not a Roman centurion, not a rapper or an astronaut. He is a middle-aged man with all the problems that come with being a middle-aged man, minus the ones having to do with money. His children don't like him, his subordinates don't like him, his time is running out, and his body can perform the tasks it once accomplished with ease only with the help of drugs. AI promises someone like him more endless role-playing. And, in his understanding, AI also renders meaningless the years or even decades of accumulated expertise that generally lend our biographies their characteristic rigidity and inflexibility.

In fact, if we try to encapsulate what AI promises, we could just say: immaturity. That may not sound particularly tempting, but loitering in immaturity also means emulating those in power. Our historical moment is characterized by the power of immaturity. Or rather: Our time is characterized by immaturity as a technique of power. As soon as a person (assuming they have the right skin color and gender) is old enough that their transgressions are no longer excused as "youthful indiscretions," they already shift into the paradigm where they are simply "part of a different generation" and therefore cannot be held responsible for their words and deeds. The power of our day is always immature. And so are the technologies that wield it.

Walter Isaacson's biography of Elon Musk is hardly uncritical of the man. But Isaacson ends his book by granting perhaps the most central proposition of Musk's power grab: immaturity is—albeit only provided you're the right kind of person—a strength, yes, even a societal good. "Sometimes great innovators are risk-seeking man-children who resist potty training. They can be reckless, cringeworthy, sometimes even toxic. They can also be crazy. Crazy enough to think they can change the world."[10] The thing with specialness is: it's the least special thing in the world to think you have it.

The Faustian bargain that technology offers us seems to consist precisely of this immaturity. In their attempts to get us excited about the potential applications of the numerous "assistants," many AI commercials seem to imagine a customer who has regressed almost to the point of infantilism. We see men in their mid-thirties "asking" Gemini how to cook pasta or what kind of restaurant would be suitable for a first date. The AI agents, which are by no means identical to AI technology as such, but nevertheless represent the most effective public articulation of their promise, essentially promise only one thing: You can forget about adulthood.

If this promise sounds a lot like a curse, it's probably because it essentially turns the main threat AI poses into a positive. Because if the trends of recent years continue, AI will primarily have the effect of keeping people in a state of untrained, undetermined adolescence for longer. In Silicon Valley, the jobs falling victim to AI are those entry-level coder jobs that previously represented the first rungs of the career ladder. Whether this is due to the true potential of the technology or instead due to the self-deception of the bosses, AI is destroying that phase of life in which one gains professional experience, contributes, and makes mistakes. In which, as Hegel would say, one "determines" oneself, opens some doors, and closes others.

It is striking: We are encouraged to defer to leaders who are not fully mature, to respect men like Musk and Trump for who they might yet turn out to be. We demand impossible maturity from our young, from women, from people who aren't white. And we are encouraged to cower before technologies that are never fully mature and yet wreak immense destruction in the here and now. We are encouraged to accept the credibility of technologies that don't even exist yet, to respect the good someone's innovation *might* do one day in the far future, though right now it only unleashes destruction. All this will one day exist, we are assured. Once these things and people are less immature. In the meantime we are told to treat them as though they were already mature. This specific privilege seems to be enjoyed by two entities in our society: the young and middle-aged men who earn billions with grandiosely overpromising technologies. And those technologies themselves.

The form of impossible biography that Elon Musk claims resembles another. Today, "AI" is primarily an object of discourse. As linguist Emily Bender and sociologist Alex Hanna write, talk of "AI" consists mainly of metaphors, and talk of its capabilities of literary allusions.[11] People "ask" ChatGPT and seek "advice" from Grok. In 2025, an "AI talent studio" in London began shopping an AI-generated "actress" named Tilly Norwood to agencies in Hollywood.

When real actors protested en masse about the stunt, the talent studio quickly reverted to referring to its "creation" and its "art project." This didn't stop economist Tyler Cowen from professing his love for "Tilly" and waxing poetically about the computer program's "virginity."[12]

Such headline-grabbing stunts are—at least so far—simply anthropomorphisms, which are meant to mystify the interaction of a human being with an admittedly complex algorithm. One of the most important developers of AI, Mustafa Suleyman, expressed concern in the summer of 2025 about a rising number of cases of apparent "AI psychosis"—that is, cases in which AI's ability to mimic human discourse patterns drives vulnerable individuals into a separate reality. "There's zero evidence of AI consciousness today. But if people just perceive it as conscious, they will believe that perception as reality."[13]

"AI psychosis," however, merely intensifies the misunderstanding that all AI providers—including Microsoft, where Suleyman works—constantly encourage in users and the public. Venture capitalist (and OpenAI investor) Geoff Lewis caused a stir on X in the summer of 2025 with a set of rambling posts: ChatGPT had supposedly "helped" him "research" a massive conspiracy that had "negatively impacted 7,000 lives" and "eliminated" twelve more. In reality, ChatGPT likely just picked up on his prompts and confirmed his every unhinged idea. It's an experience you've probably had yourself if you've ever interacted with an LLM, though the consequences may have been less disturbing. Lewis's X-reported ChatGPT experience was creepy, but ultimately it's no different from what happens to a student who "asks" ChatGPT as if it were a person and then submits the resulting mass of probabilistically generated, plausible-sounding nonsense as a term paper.

Even the fears surrounding AI, or "P(doom)" scenarios in which AI gains full consciousness and begins to dominate or destroy humanity have so far been convincing primarily through allusions to pop culture and science fiction. Our AI alarmists operate with a lot less seriousness than one would expect from a proper doomsday prophet. Whether this means they don't take their own warnings seriously, or whether (as is so often the case in Silicon Valley) they believe they can buy or fabricate an individual indulgence from collective fate, likely varies from case to case.

Above all, however, the entire industry and its product constitute one gigantic metonymy. The term "AI" is used for an almost endless list of operations, often simply to spruce up the term "algorithm." At the same time, however, each of these operations is attributed to "AI" (or "the AI") in the singular. Of course, "AI" as such can do *x*, *y*, and even *z* in exactly the same way that Elon Musk can be both supernerd and stoner bro, Bond villain and hero, computer gamer and astronaut. "AI" as such doesn't exist. But if the image of "AI" didn't exist, people like Elon Musk would have to invent it. Because ultimately, it's a self-portrait. An image of oneself as an intelligence that doesn't age and doesn't have to make trade-offs, that can claim an endless set of identities and sets of expertise.

Hegel calls the error of thinking of those who refuse to categorize themselves but rather want to be everything and nothing "abstract." Abstract is that understanding of freedom that is based solely on what the individual wants right now and neglects the fact that what the individual wants right now is conditioned by objective factors. This doesn't mean one shouldn't be guided by these factors, only that such an understanding of freedom ultimately cannot distinguish between freedom and unfreedom. And making that distinction would seem rather important for a theory of freedom.

Anyone who examines the narratives we are currently told about how AI is supposed to improve the world, or even just why it is allegedly inevitable, will quickly encounter a similar abstraction. This form of abstraction used to be called the "black box." As the philosopher and physicist Mario Bunge wrote in 1963, such an analysis understands a system as a combination of inputs and outputs that "is purely external or phenomenological."[14] Does one thing happen, or something else? The "constitution and structure of the box" are deliberately disregarded.

However, the deliberate agnosticism that Bunge introduced as a methodological intervention is increasingly becoming a trick to make power unassailable. As the legal scholar Frank Pasquale argues in his 2015 book *The Black Box Society*: Data is increasingly turning governmentality into a black box. We can at least guess what the inputs of a system look like, and we live with the consequences of the outputs.[15] But whether it's a botched credit check or the hundredth supposedly random security check at the airport: In an algorithmically governed society, it is becoming increasingly difficult to ask the most important question that a subject in a liberal democracy can ask: Why?

This is often portrayed as a question of technological maturity. Our systems simply have to be better trained. Take the case of sensors that were only tested on the skin of white people and therefore failed to detect darker skin. Or the neural network that had been trained on thousands of images of cancerous lesions, and that then "diagnosed" cancer by learning that the ruler in the images indicated malignancy.[16] Both serve as reminders that ultimately, it is still humans, with their blind spots and biases, who create these technologies. But in both cases, the problem was eventually resolved. The technology was simply immature. They continued testing, tweaked the code, and the problem disappeared.

This may be true regarding the individual functioning of specific systems. But the fundamental problem remains that humans create these systems and humans can manipulate them. And that the design and form of manipulation are today usually unavailable for questioning. To choose an example of a truly impressive system: Google subsidiary Waymo has been training autonomous vehicles in San Francisco since the late 2010s. Nearly a thousand of these electric taxis now roam the city. At this point, apart from their occasional murder of beloved neighborhood pets, their presence, with the rotating LIDAR on the roof and the empty driver's seat, attracts the interest only of the occasional tourist.

Waymos drive autonomously, which is one of the applications of AI. But autonomous driving also means that humans intervene. Waymo technicians sit in various control centers in the United States and the Philippines and lend a hand whenever an autonomous vehicle gets stuck. Former Waymo engineers told me that such a controller likely supervises between twenty and forty Waymo rides simultaneously, which likely means that intervention is necessary in approximately 2 to 5 percent of rides in the various markets the company has entered so far. As a passenger, what you notice in such a case is that the car stops briefly and then does something rather unusual.

What happens at that moment is the following: The remote operator in the data center doesn't take over the steering wheel, as passengers sometimes assume, but rather plots a new course for the car on the city map. I don't know why the company opted for this form of human intervention. The important thing is that it opted. Behind the AI of a self-driving car, therefore, lies not only human intercession but something far more significant: a fundamental framing decision about when and how humans intervene in the system. The passenger is completely unaware of this. They drift along, whether they like it or not, in their black box.

The point, therefore, is not whether AI will eventually become more sophisticated or not. Whether AI will be able to do what its creators promise or threaten. The point is that talk of maturity deprives the public of a whole range of decisions and choices, by pretending instead that there are no decisions and choices to be made. When in fact, the maturing technology will involve more and more of these decision points. When the Irish capital, Dublin, decided to build a new subway, Dermot Desmond, the ninth richest person in Ireland, proclaimed that the government should cancel the project. After all, "AI" would make the project "obsolete" anyway. He was referring to cars from manufacturers like Waymo.

In such a statement, "AI" is used as though it were a familiar and agreed-upon concept that—once it's fully developed—will have a clear and unambiguous effect, as it happens precisely the effect the speaker's argument requires. It will negate or render obsolete whatever decisions he dislikes. It will make inevitable the outcome he desires. Dermot Desmond doesn't address how this is supposed to happen, how exactly "AI" is supposed to implement autonomous driving and make public transport obsolete. More importantly, the Irish billionaire didn't seem to grasp what's obvious to anyone whose Waymo car has to be controlled by a data center: that even when the technology is far more advanced than it is now, its deployment isn't a given, but will depend on political, legal, and business decisions—decisions made by programmers and product designers, CEOs, regulators, and politicians. Or perhaps Dermot Desmond does know this; perhaps he's hoping that Irish newspaper readers will forget the fact as quickly as possible.

An interesting paradox of the algorithmic age is this: There is already an "algorithmic governmentality" that deals with how systems are actually used or managed. But often, "the algorithm" or "AI" is a smoke screen for something far more mundane. Because even where it says "AI" on the tin, there isn't always a lot of AI inside. The young programmers to whom Elon Musk's DOGE granted control over large parts of the US federal government are a kind of AI cult. However, anyone who looks at the actions of the DOGE team quickly realizes that their use of AI wasn't about governing, control, or categorization. It's about the media-savvy spectacle of government-like gestures. And it has more to do with how administrative systems can be communicated to the public they regulate. These two aspects are obviously linked, but they are by no means identical. In DOGE's arsenal, "AI" functions as a buzzword that essentially says: We're in control, don't ask any further questions.

DOGE's pitch to a right-leaning audience was this: AI and algorithms will eradicate all "deep state" actors within the federal government, as well as those who are "woke," and replace those who, according to Musk and Trump, owe their positions solely to "DEI." DOGE's actual method seems to have consisted of "asking" ChatGPT leading questions about various government offices and projects, which really isn't functionally different from using Ctrl+F in an Excel spreadsheet and randomly entering terms that suggest a person is not white. AI once again reveals itself as a fetish object, behind which far more banal social relationships, prejudices, and fears are concealed.

Who knows what other risks AI will pose to our democracy? At least for now, the real risk to our politics doesn't stem from the technology itself, but from the blathering about it. The invocation of "AI" allows for one thing above all: instead of a tyranny of algorithms, we suffer under a tyranny of cliché. In a reality cobbled together from the internet's data deluge, by machines primarily intent on manipulating sources so that no one can hold their creators accountable for copyright infringement, governmentality is incapable of looking to the future. Instead, it can only ever draw from the most mediocre and intellectually lazy things that humans have posted online in the last forty years.

With Elon Musk and X, we have seen what happens when a person whose brain has been completely ruined by social media assumes decision-making power. Thanks to Musk's DOGE foot soldiers, the USA experienced something very similar with AI. We have known for a while that historical developments always occur twice. But perhaps we've been too kind in thinking that it was first as tragedy and then as farce. Perhaps we need to amend: first as tragedy and then as slop.

SIX

Creeps

When you find yourself giving a lot of interviews about Silicon Valley—which is one of those things that tends to happen when you write a book with a title like *What Tech Calls Thinking*—you frequently encounter a question like: "How does this go together?" Young men in T-shirts on e-bikes who are nevertheless right wing? Neurodivergent computer nerds threatening to beat each other up in MMA bouts? A gay kid of immigrants bankrolling the far right? How does that go together?

What power Silicon Valley has been able to amass in the last twenty years (piled on top of the considerable power it had accrued previously) has at least in part to do with the fact that traditional categories have had some difficulty placing these companies and their leaders. In truth, there is no contradiction whatsoever contained in the questions I already posed. What these questions show is, I think, the superannuation and inertia of our political categories.

This is certainly the case when it comes to gender. Whether it's Mark Zuckerberg, midway on the journey of his life, embracing the virtues of the gym bro lifestyle, or Peter Thiel and JD Vance embracing gender traditionalism, or Elon Musk's cult leader pretensions: you can see why people might be surprised how so much gender and sexual anxiety goes together with what is often understood as a uniquely sexually progressive part of the world.

But gender points to an even bigger political mystery: How to understand the alliance between a libertarian, even libertine, tech culture, and traditional values of conservatism. Our media and commentators struggle with this question because they tend to dismiss gender as a side issue and a "culture war" that distracts from the "real thing" (money and power). But gender, of course, has a lot to do with money and power. The overlap between traditionalists like the "New Right" movement's Joseph Anton and Adrian Vermeule on the one hand and libertines like Elon Musk and Uber CEO Travis Kalanick on the other exists because they actually feel the same about dominance: that it is what makes a man, and that it is there to be exercised over women. Journalist Moira Donegan describes the first category of misogynists as "preachers," the second as "creeps."[1]

Donegan's point isn't that creeps are somehow new. Rather, she's interested in showing why the tech industry's thinking is so compatible with a traditional gender conservatism that can appear so different, at least on the surface. The priest wants to ban women from taking birth control, the creep banishes them into pornographic memes. But both agree that women (as well as trans and nonbinary people) have a very specific place in society. And for both, it is the essence of masculinity to put them in their place. This is what makes the ideology of the tech world so compatible with a traditional gender conservatism that, at least on the surface, differs so markedly from it.

Kate Manne has outlined the manifold strategies by which misogyny denies women their full humanity by entitling men to admiration, care, affection, knowability, and control.[2] This is where gender politics intersects with governmentality: It is a strange feature of the power of technology that it never truly confronts the people and things over whom it exerts power. It is allergic to being confronted with the consequences of its own actions. Indeed, many technology entrepreneurs seem to regard the very existence of consequences as a form of oppression. The way they conceptualize this form of irresponsible domination, which operates in cheerful ignorance of what it controls, is clearly gendered. It is creep power.

Masculinity is not the same as being or presenting male. It is a cultural code that can be inhabited by people of any sex. But creepiness is oddly gender specific. I am not aware of many female creep figures in media. In media and popular lore, the female creep is instead a hysteric, a psycho, an impostor. Elizabeth Holmes is probably every bit the sociopath Mark Zuckerberg is. But when we get a miniseries about Holmes, Amanda Seyfried plays her as an increasingly panicked deer in the headlights. The glowering, malevolent performance that Jesse Eisenberg gives as Mark Zuckerberg in *The Social Network*, and which performer after performer has aped when portraying a titan of Silicon Valley, appears to be almost exclusively a male preserve.

Curtis Yarvin was born in 1973, and he is largely a product of the gifted-track industrial complex. Skipped grades, young and gifted programs, IQ studies. The institutions where eugenics hid out while it was briefly uncool to talk about eugenics. As Quinn Slobodian writes, Yarvin remained "attached to the idea of the cognitive elite as an adult."[3] Democracy, to Yarvin, seemed poorly suited to recognizing those who were special as special.

Yarvin graduated Brown at nineteen years old and went on to pursue a PhD at Berkeley, which he would eventually abandon. Like many dropouts, he stayed close to the university and still lives in the East Bay. He worked at various start-ups, developed the peer-to-peer platform Urbit, and founded the start-up Tlon in 2013, named after the short story by Jorge Luis Borges, "Tlön, Uqbar, Orbis Tertius."

It was in a way a pretty typical tech career, with all the gaps and sabbaticals afforded by the astronomical salaries, copious investment cash, and relaxed work culture of late 1990s/early 2000s tech. What set Yarvin apart was his activity as a political essayist. Starting in the late aughts, Yarvin attracted notice for a blog he wrote under the pseudonym Mencius Moldbug. In his posts, Yarvin developed an eclectic neoreactionary philosophy: a quasi-monarchical system gathered around a leader/CEO.

"Democratic politics proper is basically dead," Yarvin claims. It has been undone by a cabal of deep state actors and mainstream media that he dubs "The Cathedral." He advocates politics as "a cold war" with clear friends and enemies, and a "hard reset" of society that alone will be able to dislodge the forces of The Cathedral.[4] He doesn't seem to believe that the hard restart can be achieved without violence.

Much has been written about Yarvin's ideas in recent years. Yarvin's essays—which first appeared on his blog, now on his Substack *Gray Mirror*—are long, they hurtle from one idea to another. Stylistically, his short, apodictic sentences manage to be both sententious and curt. They drip with self-regard and pathos, while being grammatically sparse. They delight in big, bold statements that amount to just wiping all the china off the table. The style is somewhere between a meme and warmed-over Marcus Aurelius; the substance is somewhere between a usenet poster and warmed-over Carl Schmitt.

Yarvin's posts owe an obvious debt to Schmitt, the authoritarian legal theorist and "court jurist" of the Nazi state. Leftist critics like pointing to this connection and emphasize continuities with Nazism. Which is the entire point, for people ranging from Stephen Miller to JD Vance, of quoting or alluding to Schmitt. They want to be seen doing it, and they want you to yell about them doing it. They may also agree with Schmitt, or think they agree. But it doesn't seem, as a rule, that they've gotten very far in their reading of the man's books. Schmitt to them is a fount of very quotable propositions you can bandy about like a nugget you found in a stream. And each nugget is sure to get a reaction.

Their invocations of Schmitt often feel like trolling, meant to "trigger the libs." It's neither a misappropriation nor a misunderstanding of Schmitt, since the jurist was a bit of a troll himself. Schmitt was a master of the grabby first sentence, curt, bold, and impossibly big. Perhaps most famous among them: "The sovereign is the one who decides on the state of exception." Like Schmitt, Yarvin favors dictatorship over democracy; like Schmitt, Yarvin thinks that all politics is founded on the distinction between friends and enemies; like Schmitt, Yarvin believes that liberal politics and democracy are incapable of meeting the crisis that liberal politics and democracy inevitably bring about. But above all Yarvin seems to like Schmitt's way of arguing—sweeping statements almost too big to truly double check.

While he has been writing and gaining attention for his writing since the aughts, Yarvin broke through with a wider public as part of a whole raft of far right thinkers who came onto the scene via the internet sometime around the 2016 election. What is less obvious in the case of Yarvin than in the case of, say, conservative commentator Jordan Peterson, is that there is a particular style of masculinity being modeled in his missives. The hard-nosed, epigrammatic style, the insistent talk about "total victory" and war metaphors, the highly selective pilfering and adaptation of pop culture, feel tailor-made for a particular kind of man. A man very much like Yarvin. One who senses that he is better than others and who looks in frustration at a world that doesn't, or doesn't sufficiently, reflect that sense back at him.

In 2022, profiles of Yarvin appeared in various English-language newspapers and magazines. A Substack post from April 2022 is addressed to people who have read those media profiles and are now perusing his newsletter: "If someone sent you this link, someone thinks you are looking for something." Yarvin treats a link to a Substack post as a gesture of election, like a Yale student getting tapped for Skull and Bones. Yarvin was likely channeling Laurence Fishburne's Morpheus from *The Matrix*, though to be fair similar lines have been uttered by every cult leader in history.

And, like every cult leader in history, Yarvin is here to tell you that you can still walk away: if his thought seems "boring or weird or dangerous or something—this stuff is probably not for you. That's fine. It's not for most people. And there are many senses in which it is dangerous! Most people are what they are: imperfect beautiful mere human beings who should stick to the airport bookstore."

This, ladies and gentlemen, is what we in the business call a classic "neg." This term comes from the toolbox of "pick-up artists," male influencers who want to teach other men how to best pick up women, and refers to a manipulation in which a neutral or even flattering statement is intended to undermine a woman's self-esteem. Yarvin treats his prospective readers much the same way, even though he seems to be imagining them as men: You *could* walk away like a simpleton who likes airport books. You *could* decide that Yarvin's thought is dangerous like some kind of libtard cuck. Like so much of Jordan Peterson's output, this is a special boy telling you that you too are a special boy. The real aim, of course, is to bind the person in question to oneself through disidentification: No, that's not me! I'll keep reading!

As with the "negs" of pick-up artists, Yarvin's approach is both about manipulating others and about protecting himself against rejection. How often prominent pick-up artists actually succeed with their dubious party tricks is questionable, to say nothing about the losers who adopt their seduction techniques and deeply misogynistic view of women. And so, pick-up artists spend a lot of time explaining to the "special boys" that if women don't recognize their specialness, then those women aren't worth their time in the first place. Yarvin's rants also always include the possibility that the reader will reject them. He expends great energy explaining why the rejection he so persistently addresses is so incredibly irrelevant to him.

Is Yarvin serious with all this? That's really hard to tell. Because his Schmittian decisionism coexists at all times with the snarky masculinity of the troll, delighted that you got triggered. He clearly regards himself as a latter-day Jonathan Swift. But perhaps it would be more accurate to say that Yarvin is so deeply steeped in meme and shitposting cultures that the borders between what is his actual opinion and what is trolling can be hard to draw. He closes the paragraph I cited above with the phrase: "Would you like to know more?" This is an allusion to the 1996 film *Starship Troopers* where it accompanies indoctrination into an autocratic society.

Yarvin is, in fact, trolling a troll: back in the 1990s, director Paul Verhoeven turned the jingoistic science fiction novel about American greatness, *Starship Troopers*, into a movie that slyly suggested that such jingoism was in truth deeply fascist. Generations of viewers delighted in a film that seemed to celebrate the derring-do of the human forces while not-so-secretly presenting those human forces as the bad guys. In a move that you find quite often among the alt right, Yarvin reidentifies with the fascists.[5] And if it were so, he asks. If American jingoism was in the final analysis identical with fascism, would that trigger you?

But the identification and the violence that you find in his rhetoric are always also ironic. And in this regard he has proven quite influential: so many of those now in charge fixate on total power, while also never being entirely serious about total power. Watching JD Vance and Elon Musk do politics, you get a sense of Yarvin's thought in action: a quest for power and domination so fully ironized that it never has to look itself in the face. The sovereign may get to decide the state of exception; the troll gets to live in it always.

But for all of the troll's bravado Yarvin displays, one place where he seems capable of immense sincerity is in pitying himself. "I maybe the most misquoted philosopher alive," he once complained in a court filing. He seems convinced that leftists are plotting to kill him. His son, he has claimed elsewhere, "has been punished for being my son, including last-minute exclusion from a competitive youth soccer team due to his name." (What youth soccer coach would be aware of Mencius Moldbug's real name is another question, but people around Yarvin seem quite convinced that he is transcendently famous.)

Whoever has watched self-declared "free-speech absolutist" Elon Musk censor content critical of him, or JD Vance construct threats out of nothing while dashing off a constant stream of threats himself, has seen this form of creep masculinity in action: they can be quite sensitive, even maudlin, in assessing things happening to them, but then are capable of seigneurial aloofness when doing the same things to other people.

Yarvin persistently draws red lines that he himself would never adhere to and openly uses fascist vocabulary and metaphors that he feels no obligation to defend. It is precisely this combination of decisionism and unseriousness that makes Yarvin's rhetoric a lodestar for the Trump administration: fascist vocabulary that is meant to be both ironic and serious, in service of norms that one would never adhere to oneself, but which one indignantly demands of others.

Yarvin's influence has not been that of a popular thought leader. It has been mediated most decisively by the fact that a few powerful men were very impressed with him. To trace Yarvin's career as a Nazi whisperer essentially means tracing a web of male homosocial friendships. Blake Masters, Peter Thiel's ghostwriter and multiply and unsuccessfully Thiel-funded Senate candidate, first made the connection between Thiel and Yarvin. Alt-right gadfly Milo Yiannopoulos and Yarvin saw themselves as "coaches" in Thiel's radicalization. Through Thiel and Musk, Yarvin's thought influenced current vice president JD Vance.

You'll notice that women are missing from this web. But perhaps it's better to say that they connect these men through their absence. Because at every step along the way these men found each other and found common cause with one another by banishing women, or even "the feminine." In spite of a culture warrior past, by 2009, Peter Thiel was regarded as a fairly standard Silicon Valley libertarian. That's the year he wrote a blog post for the Cato Institute that suggested that extending the franchise to women had set the country on a disastrous path of government control and welfare state, which "rendered the concept of 'capitalist democracy' a contradiction in terms."[6]

While he walked back some of the obvious implications of what he had written, the interview was a signal flare. Here was a man willing to say that in order to have the kind of capitalism Silicon Valley wanted, one might have to drown democracy in the bathtub. And he made the point, significantly, by pointing to voting rights for women. For men who claimed to be libertarians but actually thought in terms of stark hierarchies, essays like Thiel's showed that there was in tech a constituency not just for the idea that men were better coders than women, but for the broader idea that men were naturally women's superiors.

In 2014, Thiel and Blake Masters published the book *Zero to One: Notes on Startups, or How to Build the Future* and began promoting the book. They were worried about being asked by various interviewers how to increase the number of women in start-ups, and they turned to Yarvin for an idea of what to say.

Yarvin's suggestion was simple: increasing the number of women is nonsense, start-ups should recruit only the best, and the best were obviously men. Thiel and Masters were impressed with Yarvin's no-holds-barred style—a friendship began. On Election Day 2016, Yarvin sat on Thiel's couch in San Francisco and watched Donald Trump win the presidency for the first time.

This process, like so many things having to do with backlash politics, has accelerated enormously. Elon Musk's radicalization, significantly promoted by Thiel and Yarvin, appears to have been triggered at least in part by his daughter Vivian Wilson's coming out. In early 2025, Mark Zuckerberg announced on Joe Rogan's podcast that he thought that "masculine energy I think is good" and that it was a problem that "corporate culture is really trying to get away from it."[7] After years during which a woman (Sheryl Sandberg) had been in charge of Meta, he told Rogan that "a culture that celebrates the aggression a bit more has its own merits that are really positive." The large charitable foundation he and his wife established, the Chan Zuckerberg Initiative, promptly withdrew from all the areas in which it had long been active, such as education and health care. These areas seemed, according to *The New York Times*, "too political" for the Zuckerbergs. Instead, they turned to supporting "science" and AI. It is probably no coincidence that this also represents a withdrawal from areas of interest of Zuckerberg's wife, Priscilla Chan, a physician. Zuckerberg's obsession with masculinity seems to consist primarily of destroying what the women around him value.

It's not as though these homosocial approaches ignore women. In a sense, they seem to be able to think of little else. Instead, they simultaneously evoke women, gender, the feminine—and banish them.

Alice (not her real name) founded a start-up while still in college. She moved to the Bay Area, worked at Google, and later married a high-ranking Facebook executive. She was always critical of her own industry, but shortly before the pandemic, she realized that she and her profession had completely diverged. Today, she works as a bartender in San Francisco and, on her days off, is writing a novel about the tech industry.

The bar where she works is downtown, within walking distance of many of the towers that were built in the late 2010s and now house Salesforce, Slack, Facebook, and Google. In her new job, she entertains many colleagues from her old one. She told me that one evening she started chatting with a small group from an AI start-up that was apparently in town to pitch an investor. Like a good bartender, she asked questions and played along with her little jokes between rounds. Until she made a joke about AI that made it clear she was an expert. She says the shock showed on the men's faces. "How do you know that?" they asked her.

There are plenty of people like Alice in San Francisco. People who were fed up with tech, or who found that tech no longer wanted them. Who had become wealthy enough to find something new, or who simply wanted more out of life. What Alice discovered that evening (and on many evenings since) is that many in the tech industry have an intuitive, yet all the more keen, sense of the boundaries of their sociotope. A young woman like Alice, impressively tattooed and nonwhite, especially a young woman who served them Cuervo shots and mixed good drinks, isn't part of it to them. And the suspicion that she might speak their language, know their world, comes as a shock, almost a betrayal. In other words: These people understand their own industry as both dominant and esoteric; everyone must be in its thrall, but not everyone can be allowed to be part of it.

I know many Silicon Valley dropouts—former programmers and start-up founders who now run boutiques or nonprofits—and many report precisely this phenomenon.

The figure of the Silicon Valley creep has to do with both the inside and outside of this industry, which is also a pretty tightly networked community. There's a form of male dominance behavior that conveys to women within the industry how they fit in. And so the second aspect of the Silicon Valley creep has to do with women as a play token, as "NPCs" ("Non-Player Characters"), as video gamer language has it. Part of creepiness is a set of behaviors that assigns women their place outside, on the margins, in virtual space.

Silicon Valley has always been male-dominated. Ever since the gaggle of engineers nicknamed the "traitorous eight" left Shockley Semiconductor Laboratory in 1957, symbolic patricide was part of Silicon Valley, but so was male bonding. There is a famous photo of the traitorous eight from the late 1950s, taken on the terrace of their new company, Fairchild Semiconductor. The men are wearing jackets and ties, but they lounge comfortably on garden furniture, a bit like Sinatra's Rat Pack. They are clearly fond of one another.

But although masculinity consistently dominates in Silicon Valley, this masculinity is not constant. No, masculinity here is always reinventing itself or changing over time. An oedipal moment always resonates. Both the runup to and the immediate aftermath of Donald Trump's second election in the fall of 2024 saw frequent invocations of the figure of the "Silicon Valley Bro." In truth, 2024 revealed a new version of the Silicon Valley Creep. What is the difference? "Bros" start from a presumption of male sociability without reflecting on its sources; their aversion to women has a community-building effect. "Creepiness," on the other hand, is lonely. When the creep turns to his own masculinity, he finds little commonality in it with other men. Even if the creep attempts to establish community and solidarity with other men through his masculinity rituals, as a creep, he is always alone, an opponent of other men, and preoccupied with himself. "I'm a creep, I'm a weirdo," runs a line in the Radiohead song that director David Fincher used in the trailer for *The Social Network* in 2010. "I don't belong here."

Precisely for this reason, the creep's gestures of domination are primarily desperate attempts at self-control. From Silicon Valley's interest in Jordan Peterson's "philosophy" to the cult of eternal life, "biohacking," "looksmaxxing," and endless cosmetic surgery: it's no longer about optimization, but rather a desperate attempt to master one's own creatureliness. When this form of self-optimization encounters others, it tends to make victims of those others.

For several years, media couldn't seem to get enough of Bryan Johnson, the "tech entrepreneur" who wanted to "live forever" and the bizarre and involved practices he engaged in to reach that goal. His strangely lizard-like face, often sporting a "Don't Die" T-shirt (the title of a Netflix documentary about him) was emblazoned on front pages across the United States and indeed the world. These were typically "rich man doing eccentric things" stories. The daily routine Johnson allegedly underwent—starting with, but hardly confined to, swallowing 111 pills per day—was something hardly any mere mortal with a day job could replicate.

But it soon became clear that Bryan Johnson wasn't an idle rentier who freely chatted about his eccentricities. He was an entrepreneur looking to get rich (or richer) off the credulity of others. Today, Bryan Johnson seems to have left the front pages and is primarily present on Instagram, where he promotes his "Blueprint Longevity Mix" in endless advertisements. Gone are the 111 pills, the baseball cap that lasers his scalp, and the daily stool sample. Now, as luck would have it, anyone can slow aging with this one weird trick. The aloof Silicon Valley recluse had revealed himself to be a very different, quintessentially American type: the huckster, the scam artist. And those to whom he had offered himself as an ideal turned out to be a complementary and equally quintessential American type: the mark. The creep's masculinity is always in question, which is why he reassures himself of it by way of stool samples, wearables, and, in Johnson's case, a penis monitor to fend off nighttime erections. This, to put it mildly, makes him vulnerable to quackery. And, conversely, it makes him the perfect quack.

Diets and miracle cures that promise eternal youth and beauty have existed since time immemorial. The quackery that Silicon Valley has brought into the (especially digital) world differs in that it is primarily aimed at men. From Elon Musk to JD Vance: cosmetic surgery, microdosing, dopamine fasting, and nootropics feed off the same gendered anxieties as diet pills and weight loss regimens did previously. Except that they are implicitly targeted at Silicon Valley men.

When women get caught up in this vortex, they often end up as pawns or onlookers. Or as service providers. Mandy (not her real name) has been working as a dominatrix in a San Francisco dungeon for years. Her clients include lawyers and investors, of course, but the majority of her clientele is from Silicon Valley. Some clients, Mandy says, even drive from Palo Alto to San Francisco just to be whipped or kicked in the balls on Leavenworth Street.

"It feels like 75%" of her clients, Mandy says, want to be humiliated in a very specific way: by reference to other men. "If you call them a 'bitch' or a 'cuck,' they're happy. But if you call them a cocksucker, their eyes really light up." The studio where Mandy works is less than a mile from the Castro. Nowhere in the United States would it be easier to live a normal gay life. But in fact Mandy doesn't believe that these men are "actually" gay. No, she suspects that their sexuality, even when it involves women, has other men in mind. Women are intermediaries.

SEVEN

Compounds

Ellen Pao first joined Kleiner Perkins, one of Silicon Valley's most distinguished venture capital firms, in 2005. At the time, fewer than 6 percent of VCs were women. By the time she published her book about her time at Kleiner Perkins, 2017's *Reset*, that percentage had not budged by even a percentage point. During her time at the VC fund, according to her later lawsuit, Pao experienced a deeply masculinist culture seemingly designed to keep women out. From assignations with CEOs at strip clubs to dinner table conversation about favorite prostitutes and porn stars, the female body served as a medium through which contracts were concluded and friendships cemented. Actual women, including those in nominal leadership positions, seemed entirely out of place in this courtship dance.

Though her suit against Kleiner Perkins ultimately failed, the next years saw a number of similar lawsuits alleging a similar corporate culture at firms, like Facebook and Twitter. Pao's book describes a world that runs on masculinity because it runs on narcissism. At firms like Kleiner Perkins, investment was something like a dating game where middle-aged men gave money to young men in whom they recognized themselves. Pao tells the story of the young CEO of "an oil tech company" who got partners at Kleiner to pour several rounds of funding into his venture, which then went belly-up in a most spectacular fashion. "I think," Pao writes, "all the guys just wanted to be him; failing the advent of any Freaky Friday life-swapping technology, they would at least relish the opportunity to give him many hundreds of millions of dollars."[1]

This system runs on mutual recognition but has its obverse in deliberate nonrecognition. In 2013, Gurbaksh Chahal, CEO of the online ad company Radium One, was arrested in San Francisco and charged with forty-five felonies. A video recorded by an indoor camera in his condo showed Chahal beating and kicking his then-girlfriend 117 times in the span of half an hour, as well as attempting to smother her with a pillow. Chahal received a lenient sentence and was put on probation, a probation he violated in 2016 in a separate incident of domestic battery. That same year he joined the venture capital firm NIN Ventures. When asked about their new hire's history, NIN Ventures' CEO (a woman) said on a panel that Chahal had been a "gentleman" in their interactions. The video, and the woman in it, seemed not to register. What Kate Manne has described as "himpathy" gets pushed to an extreme in Silicon Valley: Chahal's victims didn't even register as people to ignore or divest from.[2]

In 2014, the blog Valleywag published emails by SnapChat CEO Evan Spiegel. They were from his time as a brother at Stanford's Kappa Sigma fraternity. The emails were all about "tits," "bitches," sexual humiliation, and other fraternities being "gay." Spiegel immediately apologized for writing "idiotic emails during my fraternity days." What made the Valleywag revelations so spicy was that Kappa Sigma wasn't just a relic of Evan Spiegel's long-ago (as in: two years ago in 2014) fraternity days. The problem was that the erstwhile Kappa Sigma was then much of SnapChat's C-Suite.

James Damore's "Google Memo" ("Google's Ideological Echo Chamber") was written in 2017. It proceeds from a place of putative egalitarianism: Damore, then a Google engineer, thought that attempts to bring more women and minorities into the company was discriminatory against the white men who made up most of the company's staff. And he argued that the obvious racial and gender monoculture at Google was not evidence of disparities or bias. Rather, it was evidence of biological differences between the sexes. Women gravitated "naturally" away from higher math, from assertiveness, and from "things"; they tended toward "neuroticism," "agreeableness," and "empathy," preferring to work with people.[3] Women working within Google, and tech more broadly, were understandably outraged. While it was hardly the point then, it is worth noting now, nearly ten years later, how much Damore's picture of the sexes amounted not just to a waving-away of discrimination and sexism as a structuring force in society—it also amounted to so much male self-soothing. The portrait of women in the Google memo is one thing; the collective portrait of men sounds frankly delusional.

Much has been written in recent years about Peter Thiel's fascination with the thinking of his former teacher, René Girard. Girard taught that all desire was mimetic, that the qualities that might attract us to a person or thing are not qualities of that person or thing but rather reflections of the desire on the part of another desiring subject. You might be forgiven for thinking that this makes every human being ever sound like they're starring in a John Hughes high school movie and are vying for the popular girl. It's not that we don't recognize the dynamic Girard describes, it's just that the dynamic Girard describes sounds inherently parochial. It feels like it's true for some very specific places. Silicon Valley turns out to be one of them.

Silicon Valley's fascination with Girard's way of thinking can also be explained as follows: it sees the object of desire as essentially a projection screen with no apposite qualities of its own. The alleged triangular relationship is in truth a relationship between two people. The object itself has no qualities that do not arise from the two desiring subjects. It is not far-fetched to think that this interpretation of the world is so successful in Silicon Valley because it describes quite accurately the lived reality of many men in Silicon Valley. A world in which only other subjects, more or less identical to oneself, are real, and in which the objects of desire are less than. As a description of reality, mimetic theory is deeply strange. As an involuntary self-portrait of our new ruling caste's view of that reality, it is indispensable.

"Genius," "gentleman," but also "manchild": those are the obvious building blocks of Silicon Valley self-mystification. But it's easy to miss that terms like these build bridges between men, and that they ferry their intercourse above the heads of women. A VC recognizes the genius of a founder because he feels reminded of himself. A relationship forged over keg stands at a fraternity house spawns a billion-dollar company. Whatever the details of Ellen Pao's employment at KP, or Tina Huang's at Twitter, or Chia Hong's at Facebook, whatever employment lawyers and the legal system make of them: what these women were experiencing was being de-subjectified. They were turned into brute matter, or else white noise, in someone else's experience. They were made to stick out and become invisible at the same time.[4]

"Creep," though less flattering, is one of those mystificatory terms as well. The sneering disregard of Jesse Eisenberg's version of Mark Zuckerberg in *The Social Network* is not meant to be endearing. But the film's portrait and Zuckerberg's own self-conception likely coincide in one important point: he's different from those around him, something film-Mark mostly demonstrates by treating others (above all women) like crap. But here's the thing: men who treat women this way are exceedingly common. The creep is the ordinary somehow rendered extraordinary. We're asked to find something singular in something depressingly pedestrian.

In one passage in her book, Pao reproduces the ad she responded to when applying to Kleiner: among the job requirements was "an engineering degree (only in computer science or electrical engineering), a law degree and a business degree (only from top schools), management consulting experience (only at Booz Allen or Bain), start-up experience (only at a top start-up—e.g., one funded by Kleiner—and only in corporate, business, or product development), enterprise-software experience (only at a big established company known for training employees, like Microsoft) . . . oh, and fluency in Mandarin." And yet it was the series of interchangeable twenty-two-year-old flimflam artists with business ideas like "Uber for oil wells" that were Kleiner Perkins's special boys.

You might be tempted to chalk up the corporate culture at Kleiner Perkins to finance industry bros rather than Silicon Valley nerds. And indeed, it seems more unlikely that favorite porn actresses would come up among a bunch of programmers than within just about any other male-dominated corporate setting in the United States. Nevertheless, what would come up are other subcultures: various fan communities, favorite message boards, and video games. And it turns out that these mediating cultural objects too are subject to serious gender policing. Sure, the conversation around the dinner table was premised on the fact that Ellen Pao was unlikely to be a fan of Jenna Jameson. But if it had been a conversation about video games, she would have been told—or at any rate given to understand—that she wasn't really qualified for that either. Not that she wasn't a fan, but that she wasn't a real fan.

Kleiner Perkins' CEO once described the kind of founder the firm liked to fund as follows: "White, male, nerds who've dropped out of Harvard or Stanford—and they have absolutely no social life." The image of the nerd has always been male-dominated. And it has been both one of male impotence and dominance. This image of course stands in blatant contradiction to reality, where women, trans and cis, as well as nonbinary people naturally gravitated to the gender fluidity that nerd culture readily accommodates. But on screen, in comic books, and in the popular imagination, the image of the nerd is that of a boy deficient in his masculinity. But who crucially regains his masculinity by, well, dominating a woman.

The term *nerd* had existed throughout the 1960s and '70s, but its breakthrough happened around the same time as another breakthrough that would come to be associated with the figure: the home computer. There are as yet no home computers in the Nerds sketches on SNL, which otherwise establish several features that would accompany the nerd figure from here on out: nasally voices, huge glasses, eyewear retainer straps, and a lack of vocal control. But it was arguably *Revenge of the Nerds* that fully established the template.

Girl nerds were part of both the SNL sketches and the *Revenge* franchise. But above all, girls were prizes, totems of masculinity regained. The *Revenge* movies are unwatchable today because many of the "pranks" the boys of Lambda Lambda Lambda pull are essentially acts of sexual assault. In John Hughes's *Sixteen Candles*, the jock Jake and the nerd Ted make peace when Jake allows Ted to "take home" his passed-out girlfriend. Jocks and nerds were antipodes in terms of gender performance, but in the 1980s and onward they were able to meet on a shared neutral ground: the traffic in women. Possessing girls was, well, the revenge.

Again, whether in real life or in the media, nerd culture has never been entirely or even predominantly a male preserve. But as in our stories about Silicon Valley, the spotlight has reliably found and highlighted the boys and their struggles. And a certain type of nerd has sought, increasingly aggressively, to assign nonmale nerds a marginal, almost virtual status. They are hangers-on, posers, prizes. Not only have there been battles about keeping the mediating institutions free of women's presence and influence. Those battles have spawned some of the most troubling political currents of the last ten years. The online harassment campaign known as #GamerGate originated in 2014 as a straightforwardly misogynistic campaign to drive women out of video game subcultures.[5] Before long, the styles of argumentation, methods of coordinated harassment, and media personalities established during #Gamergate shaped the contemporary Trumpist right.

The creep, as a pop cultural figure, is usually unattached. His difficulty forming attachments is of a piece with his creepiness. And I think that, as a rule, he is young. There is a folk anthropology behind that cultural understanding, a sense of what ails the creep and what would fix him. Namely, growing older, settling down, getting a wife. Husbands are creeps in the popular imagination only when their eyes stray. As the most formative crop of the Silicon Valley elite has aged out of their twenties and into middle age, with all the embarrassing anxieties and bodily infirmities that goes with it, they have also started families, often several. And not only does it turn out that the sexist fantasy that founding a family is the cure for creepiness is quite obviously wrong. The once-solitary tech titans have proven something their preacher comrades in the Christian Right knew all along: there are plenty of way to be a creep in and through the family.

In *12 Rules for Life*, Jordan Peterson admonishes his, implicitly male, readers: "Have some humility. If you cannot bring peace to your own household, how dare you try to rule a city?"[6] Over the last few years, our media and broader public have become a lot less credulous when it comes to how these creeps run a city. We still don't pay enough attention to how they lord over their households.

In 2021, Curtis Yarvin's wife (and mother of his two oldest children) passed away at fifty from a cardiomyopathy that ran in her family. After a period of grieving, Yarvin used his Substack newsletter to solicit candidates for a new partner. He was using, he joked, the newsletter as "a giant personal ad—done with the usual Gray Mirror megalomania." So he was looking for young "reasonably pretty and pretty smart" women who "have read my work and like it" for an exploratory Zoom date.[7]

It's a pretty humanizing story as far as it goes. But, as so often with Yarvin, the framing took the story from recognizable to someplace deeply strange. He was looking for someone "of childbearing age," both "because I think life could come out of death" and because he had recently gone to a college campus and been mistaken for a college student. And "reasonably pretty and pretty smart" turned out to be an understatement of what Yarvin was looking for. The woman he ended up settling on, writer Lydia Laurenson, bonded with Yarvin over their high IQs and their youth as gifted kids.

In 2022, Laurenson and Yarvin broke up. She was pregnant, and the custody fight over their child is still ongoing. The trial documents, as well as Laurenson's interviews in the media, paint the picture of a deeply controlling man. Some of the accusations are of the type that emerges with some regularity during contentious custody battles: he kept her away from her friends, he pressured her to get pregnant, once their child was born he threatened to sue for full custody, he demanded a paternity test. The exhibits include angry texts sent via the payment app Venmo, meaning Yarvin had to pay several dollars for each insult.[8]

But others bespeak a curious allergy: an allergy to be made into discourse or an image in the same way he made Laurenson into discourse or images. Yarvin published numerous poems and essays about Laurenson, before and after they broke up. Yet he was incensed whenever she seemed to refer to him in public. He posted detailed information about his son online, including a picture, but was outraged that Laurenson gave the child his last name (as a middle name), wishing to keep him "safe."

In one incident, Yarvin, a noted master of not meaning what he says, interpreted a joke posting of Laurenson's about a "2022 West Coast Semi-Annual Antifa Leadership Summit" as a veiled death threat against him. "Thanks, that was really sweet," he texted Laurenson, "these are of course people the state licenses to practice low-level violence against people like me." He added a quote from a friend: "of course there's an element of playing with dominance" in Laurenson's post.

In a way this friend of Yarvin's puts his finger on what's unusual in this otherwise depressingly familiar custody fight: Yarvin seems to be engaged in a battle of dominance, but dominance that proceeds by description and definition. He is the one who gets to talk about Lydia, she doesn't get to talk about him. He gets to name and withdraw names. Many of his filings are unmistakably written in his voice, even though he was being represented by counsel.

Elon Musk, meanwhile, has begun to enter IVF contracts with various women. The number of his children is rumored to be approaching twenty. His reason is his professed concern about declining birthrates, and the wrong kind of people having all the babies. But simply wanting to have more children with his DNA doesn't explain the level of control Musk seeks over his progeny. He has had children through surrogacy while having children with the women he's dated. He has given sperm to women he wasn't dating without telling the women he was dating. He has begun forcing women who bear his children to sign any number of contracts, and moving the mothers of his children to the same massive compound outside of Austin, Texas. Much of the press coverage of Musk's dizzying family politics has highlighted his fixation on eugenics. And has perhaps spent too little time on the more obvious fact that Musk clearly just enjoys moving around women and children like game pieces on a board.

This form of masculinity is defined primarily by an absence: an absence of care work. In the 2010s, there was a joke that 99 percent of the business ideas that more or less talented twentysomethings pitched to investors arose from two questions: What can't Mom do for me anymore? And what will my wife do for me if I ever have one? Troll masculinity is all about not caring. Once a troll has successfully triggered you, they sit back in superior repose, sniggering at you for losing your cool. For taking them seriously. For caring. In caring you have become virtual to the troll.

The AI girlfriends and computer-generated waifus that some tech entrepreneurs surround themselves with today are just an extreme example of a dynamic in which caring and concern are excluded and relegated to the nonhuman. Caring, worrying, means the same in the age of trolls as being a loser, a nobody. For these people, work that primarily consists of caring or worrying should be automated or even abolished altogether. Disruption has always also been a description of a fundamental refusal to care.

As sociologist Jessica Calarco has put it, especially as the last remnants of America's social safety net fray, the ones who stand in for it are women. At the same time, that dependence leads to lesser rather than greater valuing of caregiving labor. On the one hand, care work makes the individual disposable, gives those who never engage in it the impression that "anyone" could do it. On the other hand, care work comes with deeply ideological ideas as to who is "naturally" suited to it.[9]

Calarco emphasizes that care work frequently imbues the individual with a certain invisibility, or rather, virtuality. Automation processes in the digital age threaten to generalize that kind of virtuality. Our technologies and their cultural remediation contain a message about what jobs could be automated away and therefore don't really "count." Even if a job cannot be automated, the fact that the average coder, founder, or funder thinks that it could has consequences. And the ambit of jobs for which this is true is, not least thanks to AI, ever expanding. The same shadowy area between automation and invisible labor is occupied by operations most users chalk up to "the algorithm" or, today, to "AI," but which, in truth, rely on overwhelmed workers in low-wage countries. Whether it is content moderation, customer service, or the operations of large language models: there are many daily interaction to which we apply the Turing test in reverse, believing we are dealing with technology when, in reality, it is still an overworked, often traumatized, human being.

When you try to describe the type of labor tech companies' business model and their self-conception devalue, discount, and disdain, you end up with jobs that go beyond what we normally think of as the "care economy" but that have something to do with caring for, or even just caring about. These are the kinds of jobs that take care of other human beings—the baristas and the servers our tech overlords seem so keen to automate out of existence. But they're also the sorts of roles that are simply minding the shop—your regulators, your doctors, your teachers.

The nihilism of the troll who wages a guerrilla war against sincerity, who uses irony to be responsible for exactly none of what they say, who primarily wants to "trigger" normal people, is of course entirely situational. In other situations, with roles reversed, our trolls are earnest people. The sensitivity with which prominent trolls like Elon Musk or Donald Trump demand the same piety for their feelings that they otherwise consider effeminate, degraded, or "woke" already shows that this removal of care is not equally distributed. There have to be two kinds of people. The ones who deserve care, sincerity, thoughtful attention. And those who do not. Those who do not, this discourse positions as women.

This has, in fact, long been an engine of the Silicon Valley start-up ecosystem. Certainly not every start-up, but many a new company with fledgling human resources and unclear distribution of duties relies on a perverse form of care work extended by the employees to their founder. In her 2020 memoir *Uncanny Valley*, writer Anna Wiener tells the story of her time at an unnamed start-up. "I felt very protective of the CEO," she writes, outlining his insecurities, his social awkwardness, his obvious need to please his parents.[10] She describes a situation in which a group of people who have work experience, who have a firm sense of workplace norms, who have graduated from college, keep giving runway to a young man who has none of those things. They are raising the man who will one day fire them.

They pity him, they want good things for him, even as he berates and bullies them. "We didn't acknowledge," Wiener writes, "that he might not want that for himself—he wasn't like us, didn't envy us, didn't care."[11] The CEO Wiener describes has perfected personal neediness as another form of labor extraction. He got others to care. And getting others to care can scale, as others outside the company—customers, media—continue extending the runway that harried early employees initially built. Is the kind of attention we now lavish on the most silly and bodily impulses of billionaires not an extension of the kind of care work Wiener describes? They feel they have an inherent right to the ministrations of our attention. And they can become remarkably petulant when those ministrations are withheld.

Petulance certainly plays a role in certain CEOs' lurch to the right. But for even longer it has animated among their set a form of masculinity dominated by the strategic denial of care—what has recently been dubbed "broicism." From eugenic thinking that treats women as pawns and brood mares, via effective altruism that seems to want to take emotional investment even out of the act of helping other people, our tech overlords delight in stoicism. It is a peculiar kind of stoicism; one that presumes that the stoic subject is, and deserves to be, at the top of every pecking order. That the care it withdraws is withdrawn from its lessers. Even before Jordan Peterson repackaged and marketed this particular blend of self-help and irresponsibility, fascination with stoicism suffused the tech industry. Erstwhile angel investor Tim Ferris wrote *The Tao of Seneca: Practical Letters from a Stoic Master.* Former advertising professional Ryan Holiday has written book after book offering stoicism as a form of life hacking. Elizabeth Holmes, disgraced CEO of the now-defunct biotech start-up Theranos, claimed that she read Marcus Aurelius's *Meditations* "over and over again."[12]

The form of stoicism that seems to succeed online and among those who build our online worlds, stands back above all else from what are, in the end, the results of its own actions. Marcus Aurelius, for them, is the avatar of a corporate stoicism, which combines holding all the power with not caring about the trappings of that power. As almost always with these people, this involves misreading the source text—not necessarily its letter, but what modern scholars almost universally agree is its spirit. Marcus Aurelius's *Meditations* are eminently quotable, but modern scholarship agrees that individual propositions in the *Meditations* are not to always to be taken at face value. They are meant to provide instruction, reminders, even therapy for the ruler's mind (who, after all, was not writing a book for any reader other than himself). But the modern-day Marcus Aurelius of course is no Roman emperor. He claims to adhere to a philosophy of self-governance that assumes he is, but also reacts with extreme tetchiness at any suggestion that he may be no more than a creep.

When President Trump established the Department of Government Efficiency (DOGE) only hours after being sworn in as president the second time, he explicitly did so with a view toward "modernizing Federal technology and software to maximize governmental efficiency and productivity." This was, in other words, an attempt to bring a Silicon Valley ethos to Washington.

The disruption that DOGE unleashed across the federal government—to say nothing of the people who depend on that government in some way—represents the apotheosis of creep masculinity. Over the first half of 2025, Elon Musk set loose an army of young disruptors on the federal government—the kind of unattached young nerds "with no social life" that previously Kleiner Perkins might have given tons of money to, but who were not usually involved in governance. The boys of DOGE made headlines with their brutal cuts, amplified, it seemed, by a complete disinterest in how the government actually worked. As one federal worker told *Wired*: "The vibe they gave was 'So, what is it that you do here?' and 'Why can't AI do that?' "[13]

Efficiency, to their mind, seemed to coincide neatly with the gendered matrix through which conservatives have looked at the federal government at least since Reagan. There are muscular, aggressive portions of the government, and those portions deserve all the money you can throw at them. Then there are effeminate parts of the government, and any money they spend is waste, or worse, fraud. Those parts that the DOGE boys regarded as feminized were largely there to help people—USAID, say, or the VA. And they were hardest hit by layoffs, canceled projects, and clawbacks of already appropriated funds.

But of course, within the various agencies the cuts too tended to target matrixes of care. Agencies with more women and minorities tended to be harder hit. Union protections that had long given federal workers an unusual measure of job security—and which were, especially in the case of veterans, explicitly framed as a government's care for those who had served the public and the country—were suddenly circumvented or disregarded altogether.

In other words, the DOGE cuts manifested above all as a crusade against care. To the vicious, twenty-year-old creeps, as to the chief creep Elon Musk, who unleashed them on the federal government, care was inefficiency, care was fraud. Having a man named "Big Balls" cutting funding for AIDS prevention in developing countries is almost pornographic in how openly it merges sexual domination and a sneering disregard for any system of mutual dependency.

And even among the federal workforce, DOGE's illegal (and usually also illogical) mandates seemed intended to rend structures of care. From one week to the next, DOGE proscribed remote working, which had been common practice in many agencies since well before the pandemic. It was likely intended as a stealth layoff, pushing people the new government didn't care about toward the exit. But in practice people will do just about anything to keep a job. The results were sudden moves, hasty childcare arrangements, desperate trade-offs. One IRS employee told *WIRED* about the woman in the next cubicle: "She was literally wailing, inconsolable, because she could not get into a childcare facility she could afford on such short notice. She literally had to choose between her little child and working."[14] Within days, the employee says, her cubicle was empty.

In its screaming obscenity, DOGE revealed what was always implicit in the figure of the tech creep: what we might call the biopolitics of the creep. The creep is a gender segregationist. He is enraged at the presence of women in positions of power, and he wants them (back) in what he considers their place. From James Damore's Google Memo to the current gendered push against "DEI," tech creeps have been obsessed with the few women in their industry—and equally obsessed with locating them inside a cordon sanitaire. Available, accessible, always paying attention, but not part of their world.

EIGHT

The Long Term

Silicon Valley has been promising us the future for so long that by now this future has its own history. Its ruins dot the landscape, its relics lie in our attics or on disks that none of our devices can read. The incredible speed of the hype cycle, the endless piling up of promises that would seem like carnival barking or charlatanism were they not so completely devoid of charm, so inextricably intertwined with power and the elite, generally make it difficult to even notice these remnants.

However much the Silicon Valley inventors may cosplay as Gyro Gearloose, it's always a historical reenactment: they're essentially impersonating inventors as they were imagined in the pop culture of their childhood. Their utopias, too, never truly left the world of adolescence behind. We, of course, don't have to follow their example. Growing older also means learning to historicize your own dreams and hopes. Whether we like it or not, we are moving into the future with Silicon Valley. This chapter traces this path with a backward-looking gaze, at the material that imposed optimism has crushed and piled up behind it.

One such ruin stands in Las Vegas. Its origin lies in a tweet by Elon Musk. "Traffic is driving me nuts," the Tesla CEO wrote on December 17, 2016. "Am going to build a tunnel boring machine and just start digging.'"[1] The tweet had the typical effect of a Musk tweet: It outlined a future of which no one really knew why it was supposed to be desirable or whether it was even attainable. But people accepted it. It was simply "the" future.

One of the most unsettling aspects of Silicon Valley is that it stifles our collective imagination of the future. Silicon Valley is sometimes portrayed as if it were filling a void: The visionaries from Northern California offer us narratives of the future that others do not, or no longer, provide. But in reality, Silicon Valley's utopias are often substitute fantasies. They're inserted in front of other fantasies and dreams in order to remove them from view. The tech industry decides what's utopian in the sense of audacious and what's utopian in the sense of mere daydreaming.

This was already the case well before the tunnel-boring machine in 2016, for example, with the Hyperloop in 2013. The Hyperloop was, strictly speaking, a revival of a project sketch from the 1960s, which in turn was based on a pneumatic tube system—an invention first used in the mid-nineteenth century. Musk resurrected the idea just as the state of California was starting to get serious about its high-speed rail project. State infrastructure projects have always been a thorn in Musk's side, so he tried to stymie a mid-twentieth-century vision of the future by revisiting the latest technological wizardry of the mid-Victorian era.

There is no Hyperloop, just as there is no underwater robot or Mars colony. The tunnel-digging Boring Company has also since been dissolved, but Musk's 2016 vision has indeed become a reality—a rather underwhelming reality. Since the end of 2021, you can ride the Vegas Loop in Las Vegas. Originally, it was supposed to be a Hyperloop, but that didn't happen. Then it was supposed to be run with Teslas: specially equipped, autonomous electric cars were supposed to speed beneath Las Vegas at 155 miles per hour.[2] The head of the Boring Company promised ten stations in the first six months of construction, then fifteen to twenty more stations per year.[3]

You are welcome to inspect what actually came of it on YouTube: initially, there were three stations at the Las Vegas Convention Center, where a driver hired by Tesla would cruise through a claustrophobic minitunnel at about 30 miles per hour. The total length of the system today is approximately 2.2 miles. Anyone wanting to use the Vegas Loop today has to take several escalators down into a converted parking garage at the Convention Center. There, they scan a QR code to call a car, because Loop cars only come on request. This is only possible between 10:00 a.m. and 9:00 p.m.; otherwise, there are no drivers and no cars. The tunnel consists of several sections with a single lane, meaning that traffic (which is reportedly extremely sparse) in the opposite direction has to wait until the tunnel is clear. The system isn't even a closed loop (one reason why autonomous driving is likely not yet possible). As of summer 2025, Loop taxis returning to the Convention Center from the new Riviera stop apparently turn into the Convention Center's regular parking garage entrance and drive from there to the Loop station.

Two points seem important in this retelling. The first thing that's striking is the staggering discrepancy between the grandiose promises and the pathetic reality. In any other business sector, such a discrepancy would mean at least the end of a company, if not the end of a career. Because Musk's Boring Company was swallowed up in the endless torrent of his hype, and because within the nimbus of the world's richest man, it's never clear what's real and what's virtual, the regulating function of reputation and public perception is essentially rendered obsolete. As is so often the case with Musk, it's a pitch where it's unclear who is actually being pitched. All his characteristic manipulation of public opinion aside, whose opinion is really at stake here? Whose opinion is still relevant enough to be manipulated?

Because unlike a bureaucrat who has to justify an overambitious train station or a long-delayed airport to an angry public, Musk conducts his ventures with a patronizing frivolity. He decides on the state of exception, and it's pretty much always in force. Because from the very beginning, a sense of unseriousness was part of the Loop project: it originated from a joke tweet as a solution to a nonexistent problem, as a duplication of a service that already existed—in this case, the Las Vegas monorail, which is itself hardly a masterpiece of urban planning, but at least it's longer than 2.2 miles and runs after 9:00 p.m.

That's the second point: One reason why we simply ignore the failures of the Boring Company, like those of the Metaverse or self-driving Teslas, and then eventually collectively forget them, is because we generally tend to talk and complain about government projects in this way. Think what you will about the California High Speed Rail, but the new system will definitely be more useful once built than the Las Vegas Loop. Even when Silicon Valley's efforts become monuments to hubris, failure, and incompetence, they are indicators of power. Because, as is almost always the case when Silicon Valley talks about itself these days, they are based on the unspoken distinction of who is allowed what.

In a September 2025 interview, Mark Zuckerberg said that Meta's investments in AI might not pay off. "If we end up having wasted a few hundred billion dollars, that would, of course, be very unfortunate," Zuckerberg said.[4]

But it was important to be involved. He considered AI "the most important technology enabling the most new products, innovations, and value creation in history." A potential $600 billion of wasted investment, he argued, was the lesser of two evils. This was six months before the company quietly sunsetted the metaverse, another 80 billion dollar investment that failed to pay off.

Skepticism toward government power can be a very good thing. But those who criticize the capacity of government have simply redirected their childlike belief in the creative potential of the central state toward private industry. They now naively believe that the future is identical with whatever the Silicon Valley tinkerers will present at the next developers' conference. More importantly, they believe that the founders' mistakes, ruins, and failures are merely minor hitches along the path to a future dominated by them. Everything the state touches gives them cause for skepticism, a sign that the nation-state and its specific form of sovereignty are on the wane. Nothing—no Vegas Loop, no metaverse, no AI nonsense clogging every communication channel—can shake their belief that the tech giant and its specific form of sovereignty represent the future.

As a rule, it's probably wise to watch out once your rulers begin planning primarily for eternity. Sure, you might be enthusiastic for a while about your leaders and their bold plans for the distant future. And then one fine day you find yourself standing next their sarcophagus in the tomb, as the covering stones close above you.

As a venture capitalist, Ellen Pao had more contact with Silicon Valley's elite than most people would wish on anyone. One of the obsessions among the superrich that particularly surprised her was "their panicky mindset." What she observed is something anyone notices who spends any length of time among them: For people who no longer have anything to worry about, they spend an incredible amount of time worrying. "They seem to subscribe to one of three theories about how the end will come: disease, robots, or—from what I could tell, this is the newest contender—race war." In his book *Survival of the Richest*, Douglas Rushkoff describes this simply as "the mindset."[5] Rushkoff emphasizes that this is far more than inconsequential eccentricity. Bunkers deep in the Eastern European forest, bizarre medical procedures, and genetic experiments may seem comparatively harmless. But the brutal extractivism of the tech elite, which manifests itself in its purest form in the AI boom—elegantly managing to steal your water, air, and the products of your labor in a single operation—is also based on the tech elite's feeling that after them there will be nothing.

How serious they are about these concerns, or whether these concerns are merely the product of deeply bored minds, is hard to say. But we will have to live with these concerns, whether we like it or not. Because, as Pao adds, "they have elaborate theories for how they will survive."[6] Normally, this involves domination: the (wealthy) individual escapes humanity's fatal fate by dominating their own body (such are the promises of eternal life made by futurists like Ray Kurzweil and Aubrey de Grey, or by pop historians like Noah Yuval Harari). Or the individual secures their survival by dominating their environment, for example, in climate-controlled New Zealand bunkers. This is how Silicon Valley governs: When it talks about the "survival" of "humanity," it means its own survival, not something as trivial as yours or that of your descendants.

Anyone who takes a closer look at apocalyptic thinking in Silicon Valley will notice that the end of the world in Silicon Valley is never the end. Apocalypse stories are always also narratives of the survival of the few. One such narrative, which has gained widespread traction in Silicon Valley, can be found at the end of an important book by the moral philosopher Derek Parfit. In *Reasons and Persons*, published in 1984, Parfit describes the following thought experiment: We must choose between three options: first, peace; second, a nuclear war wipes out 99 percent of humanity; third, a nuclear war wipes out 100 percent of humanity. Parfit argues that the third solution is far worse than the second because it eliminates "the possibility of future happiness."

However, one particular calculation within his neo-utilitarian thought experiment proved especially influential: "The Earth will remain habitable for at least another billion years. Human civilization is at most a few thousand years old. If we don't destroy humanity, these few thousand years could potentially represent only a tiny fraction of human history."[7] Longtermism, which has gained many followers among Silicon Valley's founders and investors since around 2017, is based on precisely this calculation. We are merely custodians of a legacy that will one day belong to trillions upon trillions of future humans, and we should act accordingly.

Such thinking can, of course, go hand in hand with calls for environmental protection and responsible stewardship of our planet. But longtermism stretches the future to such an extent that even a climate catastrophe seems like a mere insignificant episode. This is why longtermism enthusiasts like Elon Musk don't even bother with solving such problems anymore and prefer to work on colonizing other worlds in case our Earth is ever hit by a large meteorite (which, statistically speaking, happens every few million years).

That's the strange thing about a mindset that claims to address long-term problems but has little patience for problems that arise here and now (or even just within the next few generations). It's probably no coincidence that this way of thinking developed precisely among the superrich, and at the very moment when it's becoming increasingly clear that they are ruining our Earth as I write these lines. Everyone talks about the long term. The question is, whose long term are we talking about?

The concept of the long term, which Silicon Valley uses to justify its dominance, stems primarily from popular culture. When AI companies speak of the future (whether imparting dire warnings or brimming with hope), the narrative sounds like half-remembered films and science fiction stories. Part of the undignified nature of tech domination is that one finds oneself in a situation where one is forced to seriously warn against the "Gotham" system invented by "Palantir," a jumble of words that sounds like it came straight from my bookshelf when I was fourteen.

David Ellison, the Trump-aligned media mogul and son of billionaire Larry Ellison, helped turn Isaac Asimov's science fiction classic *Foundation* into an enormously expensive television series that has been more or less ignored since 2021 and languishes—a pretty, stately, and ultimately empty bauble—on the streaming service Apple TV+. In *Foundation*, a galactic empire slowly collapses, but a group of brilliant thinkers cracks the historical code of this collapse and tries to manage the apocalypse as carefully as possible. In 2021, Amazon Prime launched a similarly expensive adaptation of the fantasy saga *The Wheel of Time*, apparently initially spearheaded by Jeff Bezos himself. In the world of *The Wheel of Time*, a mysterious group of magical women battles a recurring destructive force over millennia. The series' cosmos—as the title suggests—is trapped in a cycle of eternal recurrence, but certain individuals are granted the power to manipulate these repetitions.

In 2024, Netflix released *3 Body Problem*, the story of a threat from space and Earth's centuries-long struggle for survival. The series is based on an ambitious trilogy by Chinese science fiction author Liu Cixin and was largely initiated by Lin Qi, a computer game billionaire from the People's Republic who was poisoned by one of the show's producers before filming began. Like *The*

Wheel of Time, *3 Body Problem* is about a world caught in endless cycles, whose inhabitants see humanity, with its comparatively rapid, linear development, as a threat. "It will be 400 years before we reach your planet," explains one virtual emissary of the aliens, "By the time we do, you will have long surpassed us." These are all shows about extremely long spans of time, and about people caught in the kinds of repetition that come with long spans of time—and those that manage to transcend it.

Are these series self-portraits of our tech elites? No, they are still primarily desperate attempts to replicate the decade-old success of *Game of Thrones*. But it is striking: unlike *Game of Thrones*, which, for all its lore and mythology, primarily drew its power from the deeply human drama generated by its sprawling and messy clans, the science fiction epics served up by the holy trinity of Apple, Amazon, and Netflix gaze into the vast distance. These series tell stories spanning millennia, in which characters and problems that would have provided material for an entire season in a conventional series are dispensed with in a single episode. It's television for the age of longtermism.

Longtermism, however, turns out to be difficult to narrate. It renders the future untellable because narratives require the dimension of human action, but on the scale Parfit introduces human action ultimately dissipates. This also means that the longtermist future is not an incentive, but rather a deterrent for narration, and ultimately action. Let's assume that the longermist view of Elon Musk is correct, and it would indeed be in the best interest of humanity for us to eventually spread across the universe. How does Musk know that this goal is better served by letting Musk build better rockets so that people can quickly leave Earth, even if millions of people on Earth ultimately perish from natural disasters, depredation, and wars? How do we know that it wouldn't be better to tax our billionaire class out of existence, provide free education to as many people as possible, in the hope that one of those educated in this way will one day invent travel at the speed of light?

One could speak here of motivated imagination. What Musk dreams of is always aligned with certain preferences. Which is what draws him to longtermism in the first place. The longtermist, like the effective altruist, can, more or less, invent the future by which he wishes to be guided. The quietism that accompanies longtermism, its tacit acceptance of existing hierarchies, is not a random output of this mode of thinking. Rather, this kind of thinking is traditionalism with a reversed thrust: Instead of one's own historical moment cowering before the overwhelming presence and claims of past generations, the future stands before it, equally unremitting and sublime. "The sun will gradually expand," Musk explained to Fox News host Jesse Watters, outlining his view of the future, "and therefore we will eventually have to become a civilization that lives on multiple planets, because the Earth will burn up."[8] So why solve problems that might threaten humanity in ten or twenty years, when the year 7.5 billion AD already has enough problems?

When someone says that we owe something to the future, it certainly has the sound of solidarity and ethics. But since men like Elon Musk seem free to invent the things they feel they are in solidarity with, in an unattainable future that even lizard-skinned Bryan Johnson will not live to see, solidarity and ethics ultimately become arbitrary in content. Peter Thiel says that his new obsession with the Antichrist forces us to "focus more on the future and set aside debates of the past." A future that can only be explained to us by tech-savvy amateur theologians like—quelle surprise!—Peter Thiel. The streaming series have that exact problem on an aesthetic level: they are so consumed by what they owe to the plots they've developed spanning hundreds of years and dozens of episodes that they fail to tell a good story in the fifty minutes we spend watching each installment.

Here's the thing, though: it doesn't seem like viewers are necessarily on the same wavelength as the creators and backers of these series. *The Wheel of Time* has been canceled, and *Foundation* and *3 Body Problem* limp along, largely unnoticed. None of these series really seems to have captured the zeitgeist. Perhaps this is also because the antihumanism of these productions extends clearly to the viewer as well. It might somewhat diminish the enjoyment to know that a cultural product perceives its own consumer only as an ant. And people who strikingly resemble its financial backers as a boot.

What holds true for Silicon Valley's plundering of the science fiction canon also holds true for other narratives these companies tell about the future. They speak of a vast expanse of time—a time frame in which, curiously enough, they nevertheless remain relevant and dominant. We, on the other hand, do not. Whether it's Elon Musk's eugenic fantasies, the panic surrounding declining birth rates, or the apocalyptic fantasies of the singularity's true believers: The future that many of Silicon Valley's powerful figures want to sell us is, on the one hand, predetermined, inescapable, a universal destiny. On the other hand, the superrich believe they can buy their way out of this universal destiny. Like

Peter Thiel looking into the apocalyptic future and seeing only people like him, their futures can feel empty and uninvolving because they are so uninterested in human action, human connection, human difference.

Conservative thinkers, in particular, have long recognized this. Roger Scruton, for example, diagnosed Derek Parfit's thought experiments with "a distinct aversion to the aspects of the moral life that suggest the entanglements that make us what we are."[9] In the case of the nuclear war thought experiment, this means: Certainly, trillions of people could come after us, but our ethical obligations primarily do not lie with them, but with people who are, at least temporally, much closer to hand. If we try to orient ourselves ethically toward people who are so far removed from our lives and our world that they are simply unreal to our understanding, there is a risk that our ethics will ultimately boil down to us simply not liking humans very much. "You would prefer the human race to endure, right?" the conservative author Ross Douthat asked Peter Thiel in a 2025 interview. Thiel's answer made some waves. Not because he said "yes" or even emphatically "no." But because he couldn't answer the question.

Giuseppe di Lampedusa described this problem in his novel *The Leopard* as follows: An aristocrat, a representative of a dying class, explains how he understands his historical responsibility: "Any palliative which may give us another hundred years of life is like eternity to us. We may worry about our children and perhaps our grandchildren; but beyond what we can hope to stroke with these hands of ours we have no obligations."[10] Conversely, one could say: A way of thinking that abandons and abstracts from the hands that we will caress during our lifetimes in favor of a largely nominal responsibility for a future whose point seems to be that it negates this interconnectedness is, in essence, simply irresponsible. Responsibility is responsibility for what is given. Responsibility for a pipe dream is narcissism with a few extra steps.

It's probably no accident that Lampedusa's protagonist describes his anxieties about the smaller, more intimate universe of hands and touches, of children and grandchildren, in conversation with a priest. When he invokes a kind of miniaturized eternity, which actually only applies to those generations whose world an individual can still imagine, he has a very specific counterexample in mind: the Church. When the Church says "eternal," it truly means "eternal." Its generations follow one another in a chain that, by its own definition, stretches to the end of time.

And indeed, many in Silicon Valley have begun to operate with theological categories when looking to the future. When Peter Thiel offers lectures in "political theology," it's not just a reference to Carl Schmitt. Whether it's AI or Trumpism: Silicon Valley looks so far into the distance that only theology seems relevant anymore. Or, to put it more cynically: It's the old trick "to lull the masses, the great lout, when they whine." Only it's no longer the soothing platitudes from heaven that are meant to placate them, but the relentless "Don't reason!" of AI.

One of the most fatal confusions that Silicon Valley has introduced into public discourse lies in the fact that descriptions of a possible future and hype are by now barely distinguishable. The AI boom that began in the early 2020s has unfolded on several levels. Certainly, there is the technology, which is poised to revolutionize or render obsolete specific industries and cultural practices. Far more relevant, at least so far, is the boom on another level: the cultural imagination surrounding this phenomenon. And then there is a third level: the Silicon Valley hype machine that plays on this cultural imagination. On this level, AI seems to have long since left the boom behind and has firmly entered bubble territory. No matter how much attention the phenomenon deserves, it simply cannot deserve as much as it receives.

From the very beginning, Sam Altman, the CEO of OpenAI, has warned of the technology he launched in almost apocalyptic terms. "We are a little bit scared," he said shortly after ChatGPT launched.[11] And followed this up with warnings that "although current-generation AI tools aren't very scary, I think we are potentially not that far away from potentially scary ones." In May 2023, he testified at a Senate subcommittee meeting warning that his technology might end civilization, kill everyone, and upend the 2024 election.[12] Somehow, also from the very beginning, he has also promoted OpenAI's products enthusiastically. In fact, his warnings about the technology and his promotion of it are at times indistinguishable. Altman is an entrepreneur—even his warnings are a pitch. Who knows, maybe AI will one day make the legal profession obsolete, but when Sam Altman warns that AI will one day make the legal profession obsolete, it's no more a statement of fact than a vacuum cleaner salesman telling you at your door that you're going to have to throw away your old vacuum cleaner. In this way our tech visionaries have colonized our future, turning it into an endless expanse of their own barely credible PR.

This pattern continues in many dominant sectors of the technology industry: The crypto industry loudly calls for more regulation but doesn't seem to actually want any. Sam Bankman-Fried, the now-convicted head of the crypto exchange FTX, among other things, reliably called for more government regulation of his industry. "That was bullshit," he clarified afterward. The reason for the bullshit wasn't, or not only, that he wanted to deceive or distract. No, by calling for government intervention and warning against his own industry, he put crypto (and FTX) on the agenda, making it a top priority. How often are we told that we have to "learn to live with" something, that it will happen "like it or not"? The Silicon Valley hype machine always also aims at this abandonment of collective will to shape the future, this defacement of society's sense of possibility. By promising us the moon, Altman's hype taught us not to believe promises anymore, indeed, not to promise each other anymore.

As a professor of comparative literature, it does not feel like my place to say what AI will ultimately be capable of and what it won't. What I can say, as a specialist in political discourse, is this: the flood of warnings and promises regarding AI currently overwhelming us closely resembles those of previous Silicon Valley hype cycles. Does this mean that this time it will turn out exactly like blockchain and augmented reality, Second Life and the metaverse, seasteading and the hyperloop? No, of course not. But what we can demonstrate—regardless of what turns out to be hype and what is a solid prediction—is how this hype cycle compares to previous waves.

And in this context, what's striking is a significant murkiness surrounding the act of making promises itself. What exactly can and does AI still promise us? From the start, even its biggest advocates were more likely to sound ominous warnings about their own product than genuinely celebrate it. When Sam Altman's OpenAI burst onto the scene, it wasn't in the usual guise of the Silicon Valley prophet of feasibility and possibility. Instead, it appeared more like a manic street preacher, ranting about the end times on a street corner somewhere.

In general, the future as Silicon Valley envisions it doesn't sound much like a promise anymore. It sounds like a threat. The world that Musk, Thiel, Altman, and others imagine is bleak and dystopian. It doesn't appear to be wielded as an incentive, but intended rather as a tool for discipline. Indeed, so much from Silicon Valley is fundamentally intended to discipline or even punish the recalcitrant human element. In many people's minds, AI is something like a vengeful god, chastising sinful flesh.

In the fall of 2025, Peter Thiel gave a lecture series at the Commonwealth Club in San Francisco. The media were excluded. The topic was one that Thiel had already discussed with the theological faculty at an Austrian university. And he had presented it at Oxford, Harvard, and the conservative University of Austin, each time behind closed doors. At the beginning of his first lecture, Thiel introduced himself as a "classical liberal who is afraid of the Antichrist." While this particular way of mixing them may be uniquely Thiel's, the combination—laissez-faire in the face of our challenges on the one hand, and panic about more or less imagined threats on the other—has long characterized the perspective of many figures in the tech industry. It lies behind their fascination with Yuval Noah Harari's historical superwide shots. It lies behind the increasingly blatant eugenics of the "MAHA" movement.

In the event, Thiel's lectures ended up being less and less about liberalism and more and more about the Antichrist. Thiel's thesis was that the Antichrist, or his "legionaries," are among us, that modern thought, in its fragmentation, can no longer grasp him, and that the danger now lies in the Antichrist precipitating the end of the world with apocalyptic warnings of doom. In certain passages of Thiel's lectures, this Antichrist wore the garb of climate activist Greta Thunberg, in others the garb of Representative Alexandria Ocasio-Cortez, and repeatedly the pallium of Pope Leo XIV. But above all, he repeatedly bore the face of tech insiders who warn against AI: "In late modernity," science has become "frightening and apocalyptic," which is why the "legionaries of the Antichrist" are promising an end to science, "like Eliezer Yudkowsky, Nick Bostrom, and Greta Thunberg, to advocate for a world government in order to stop science."

What was remarkable about the San Francisco lectures was Thiel's fundamental approach: a radically boundless concept of apocalypse. Some believed Armageddon would come from climate change, he said, others from a "collapsing population." Still others from the coming totalitarian world state. But: "If you believe that violence originates from us, then you are compelled to think that these existential risks, these apocalyptic risks, are perhaps one and the same risk." "That violence originates from us" is almost certainly a reference to René Girard's understanding of apocalypse—namely, that mutual mimetic desire drives humanity toward ever greater violence until this development inevitably leads to catastrophe. But as is so often the case when Thiel, when tech right-wingers, when Girard's disciples go fishing in the vast ocean of the world, Thiel is merely probing a shallow pond. All threats may be one. A profound thought! But before long Thiel has settled on the main threat being that the state has decided to impose a few regulations on companies in which Thiel has invested and which his friends run. A similar distortion runs through his laundry list of doomsday scenarios, where Thiel conflates threats that genuinely concern many people (the climate crisis, for example) with the whims of his eugenics-obsessed billionaire friends (such as birth rates).

Thiel clearly intended his lectures as a grand synthesis, bringing together theology, Girardian philosophical anthropology, Schmittian political thought, with observations about art history, the university and manga series the billionaire enjoys. He delivered it with the ostentatious breadth and learning of a university lecture. And yet, the dividend of his syncretism was, time and again, nothing more than theologically inflated narcissism. Regardless of who ends the world—AI or Satan, who warns against AI—it all remains within Thiel's own social sphere. When he looked to the future, he saw nothing but apocalypse, and in the apocalypse, no one but himself and his own kind.

It is one of the most remarkable notions of our time that what Silicon Valley sells us is "the future." In a certain technical sense, that's correct, but only if we remove all utopianism from the word. What kind of future is AI selling us? One of social devastation, one that is supposedly inevitable and in which many of our jobs will become obsolete.

But there's a reason why apocalypticism and propaganda regarding AI are indistinguishable. They imagine the future as a predetermined, but ultimately quite horrific, place. Similarly, Elon Musk likes to say that "space represents hope for so many people." Fine, but his vision of a space-bound future, in which generations of infertile simpletons struggle for dwindling resources in increasingly hellish cities, while the genetically and socially superior live the good life in orgy domes on Mars, seems, let's just say, anything but utopian.

This ersatz version of utopianism—the delusion that "the future" holds not a reorganization of social relationships, our time, or our biographies, but rather a slightly more powerful iPhone or a marginally optimized workflow—itself represents a retreat. It is the kind of progress promised to people who have nothing to hope for. Or whom one hopes will never even begin to hope.

But like the Hyperloop, a fantasy that exists only to limit collective imagination in another way, the distortion of hope tells us not only that true progress must be technological progress and that the petty utopianism of a better phone is true utopianism. Many writers, journalists, and thinkers inside and outside Silicon Valley, but especially those obsessed with Silicon Valley, thereby dismiss what is actually quite utopian as pessimistic, conservative, and timid.

We find ourselves in the paradoxical position that long-termism—a bizarre eugenic fantasy about the miserable demise of the vast majority of actually existing humans while a few wealthy geniuses carry on the flame of civilization into distant millennia on their private jets—is somehow portrayed as utopian and visionary. Meanwhile, the vision that humanity might find a way to live on this planet without destroying its riches is dismissed in many places as puritanism and small-mindedness. Is the idea that children will soon be free of asthma and able to drink from any body of water really so cowardly? Is the idea that humanity could thrive without everything around it dying really a betrayal of utopia? Doesn't it sound, rather, like the very embodiment of faith in the future?

Thanks to Silicon Valley, we've been taught to worry that moral crusaders will abolish our beloved gas stoves, light bulbs, and megasprawl cities, and in doing so, we fail to notice that the promises of climate activists, to name just one example, seem to fit rather well with the glades where we can hunt in the morning, fish in the afternoon, raise livestock in the evening, and be critical critics after dinner. You don't have to wish for this world, you don't have to find it realistic. But you have to admit that it sounds bolder, bigger, and more inspiring than "the rich get richer, the poor get poorer, but for some inexplicable reason, your dishwasher can communicate with your car."

This is a world that Silicon Valley has also helped to shape. Silicon Valley is the symbol and figurehead of a distortion in the concept of progress. And it's a symbol that selectively inhibits and promotes our view of the future, ultimately hemming in our capacity to collectively decide. In order to truly understand it, Silicon Valley must be understood as such a distortion. Admittedly, this is anything but easy at a historical moment when dominance seems to fall effortlessly into the laps of these corporations. When they subjugate politics and civil society. When they no longer need to concern themselves with the course of the world because they themselves seem to be the course of the world.

But it is helpful to consider their ruins and missteps, their debris and rubble. And to analyze their triumph as ruins in the making. Percy Bysshe Shelley's sonnet "Ozymandias" explores this tension: "Look upon my Works, ye Mighty, and despair!" says the statue, but after millennia, it is of course "a colossal wreck." Its displays of power—its "sneer of cold command"—have long crumbled into irony in the sands of time. The future may belong to them. But what about the long term? We must not leave that to them. And we likely won't have to. They too may find that the long term is the acid bath of whatever is dominant now.

Acknowledgments

This book began as a request from academic colleagues in both Germany and the United States to revisit some of the themes in *What Tech Calls Thinking* in light of recent changes in and around the tech sector and its entwinement with our politics. My first debt of gratitude is thus to Joseph Cermatori and the Periclean Honors Forum at Skidmore College for giving me the assignment that, in time, would evolve to be this book. Around the same time, Silke van Dyk asked me to give a talk in Erfurt on what ownership meant in Silicon Valley in the age of trillion-dollar valuations. These two lectures set me on the path to this new book.

As always, Christian Heilbronn at Suhrkamp had an unerring sense of what a book of this type would need to look like and what questions it would need to address. Erica Wetter, Alan Harvey, and the entire team at Stanford University Press were brilliant in steering this book toward a US readership.

In developing these ideas, I relied on the expertise of various friends and colleagues, in many cases bouncing ideas off them: I am indebted to the counsel of Wendy Liu, Moira Donegan, Becca Lewis, Angèle Christin, Genevieve Smith, Alison Dahl Crossley, Quinn Slobodian, Ben Tarnoff, Veena Dubal, Moira Weigel, Daphne Keller, Fred Turner, and many more. Cynthia Newberry went over several chapters with a fine-toothed comb, removed some infelicities I'd left there in translation, and had some amazing suggestions for local color, generously drawing on her decades of living around the tech industry.

I dedicate this book to my family, above all my husband and my amazing daughter River. It is the question of what world I hope to see her become an adult in that drives much of my critique of the people currently giving their own deeply warped, nihilistic, and fascistic answers to the same question.

I am indebted to my many friends who continue to work in the tech industry, and who were able to provide feedback and steer my ideas. I am additionally grateful for everyone who has spoken with me on background over the years. I think it takes a particular kind of openness to supply information that they know will likely be used in a manner not entirely supportive of how they spend their lives.

Finally, I want to thank each and every listener of *In Bed with the Right*, the podcast I am lucky enough to cohost with the brilliant Moira Donegan. Their emails, comments, Discord messages, and posts about our show continue to shape my thinking and my analysis of the present moment. I am fortunate to get to do the work I do surrounded by amazing colleagues. I sometimes can't believe I also get to do it in dialogue with thirty thousand of the most opinionated, curious, and brilliant people I have ever had the good fortune to meet.

Notes

Introduction

1. F. Scott Fitzgerald, *The Great Gatsby* (1925; Scribner, 1995), 27.

2. Cedric Thompson, "Magnificent 7 Stocks: What You Need to Know," *Investopia*, December 12, 2025, online at www.investopedia.com/magnificent-seven-stocks-8402262 (all online sources were last verified in January 2026).

3. Lyle Daly, "The Magnificent Seven Makes Up One-Third of the S&P 500—Should Investors Be Concerned?," Yahoo! Finance, October 29, 2025, https://finance.yahoo.com/news/magnificent-seven-makes-one-third-140006761.html.

4. Nick Lichtenberg, "Without Data Centers, GDP Growth Was 0.1% in the First Half of 2025, Harvard Economist Says," *Fortune*, October 7, 2025, https://fortune.com/2025/10/07/data-centers-gdp-growth-zero-first-half-2025-jason-furman-harvard-economist/.

5. Wendy Liu, "San Francisco's Billboards Aren't For You," *Bay Area Current*, July 21, 2025, https://bayareacurrent.com/the-billboards-arent-for-you/.

6. Cory Doctorow, *Enshittification: Why Everything Suddenly Got Worse and What to Do about It* (Farrar, Straus and Giroux, 2025).

7. Alex Karp and Nicholas W. Zamiska, *The Technological Republic* (Crown Currency, 2025).

8. Karp and Zamiska, *Technological Republic*, xiii.

9. Italo Calvino, *The Invisible Cities* (Harvest, 1972), 5.

Chapter 1

1. Godwin B. Steinberg and Susan Wolfe, *From the Ground Up: Building Silicon Valley* (Stanford University Press, 2002), 24.

2. Portions of this chapter have previously appeared in *Logic* magazine as "The Wealth Creators," September 30, 2021.

3. Malcolm Harris, *Palo Alto: A History of California, Capitalism, and the World* (Little, Brown, 2023).

4. Richard White, *Who Killed Jane Stanford?* (Norton, 2022).

5. Richard W. Lyman, *Stanford in Turmoil: Campus Unrest, 1966–1972* (Stanford University Press, 2009), 5. Quoted in Noam Cohen, *The Know-It-Alls: The Rise of Silicon Valley as a Political Powerhouse and Social Wrecking Ball* (New Press, 2018), 10.

6. C. Stewart Gillmor, *Fred Terman at Stanford: Building a Discipline, a University and Silicon Valley* (Stanford University Press, 2003). The university's endowment, which includes those endowed funds invested in the Merged Pool as well as other real estate assets on and around campus, was $40.8 billion on August 31, 2025, the end of Stanford's fiscal year. https://news.stanford.edu/stories/2025/10/report-investment-portfolio-value-endowment.

7. Chuck Collins, *The Wealth Hoarders: How Billionaires Pay Millions to Hide Trillions* (Polity, 2021).

8. Adam Kotsko, *Neoliberalism's Demons: On The Political Theology of Late Capitalism* (Stanford University Press, 2023).

9. Cathy J. Cohen, "Punks, Bulldaggers, and Welfare Queens: The Radical Potential of Queer Politics," *GLQ: A Journal of Lesbian and Gay Studies* 3/4 (1997): 437–65.

10. Tom Nicholas, *VC: An American History* (Harvard University Press, 2020).

11. Tim Dickinson, "Trump Megadonor Brags of Easy Access to White House," *Rolling Stone*, April 11, 2025, www.rollingstone.com/politics/politics-news/trump-donor-chamath-palihapitiya-brags-access-white-house-1235315702/.

12. Luisa Beltran, "The Top Power Players at Elon Musk's Department of Government Efficiency (DOGE)," *Fortune*, March 6, 2025, https://fortune.com/2025/03/06/doge-musk-venture-a16z-sequoia-tesla-twitter/.

13. Tweet by Stephanie Chen (@isosteph), November 13, 2020. The tweet is no longer available online.

14. Tweet by Jake Chapman (@vc), August 1, 2020, at https://x.com/vc/status/1289731289487011840.

15. Josh Harkinson, "Masters of Their Domain," *Mother Jones*, June 20, 2007, www.motherjones.com/politics/2007/06/masters-their-domain-2/.

16. Lambda School has recently been rebranded as Bloom Institute of Technology, though it is still headed by Allred and seems to continue offering AI training and web development courses. Its website can be found at www.bloomtech.com/about.

17. The interview can be found at www.youtube.com/watch?v=q_vLLrB3Pus.

18. The video of the interview from April 12, 2018, can be found on YouTube.

19. Quoted in Amanda Holpuch, "Signature Setback for Ballot Proposal to Split California into Six States," *Guardian*, September 13, 2014.

Chapter 2

1. Sean Mohanan, "I Predicted the 'Vibe Shift'—and Watched It Sweep the World. Here's What It Actually Means," *Guardian*, December 19, 2022, online at www.theguardian.com/fashion/2022/dec/19/how-can-you-spot-a-vibe-shift-that-transforms-popular-culture-ask-me-i-literally-invented-the-term.

2. See David Golumbia, *The Politics of Bitcoin: Software as Right-Wing Extremism* (University of Minnesota Press, 2016); Dominik A. Leusder, "How Republicans Fell in Love with Crypto," *Jacobin*, August 10, 2024.

3. Paul Graham, "How to Think for Yourself," https://paulgraham.com/think.html.

4. "Leaked Zuckerberg Audio: 'You Go to the Mat and You Fight,'" BBC, October 1, 2019, www.bbc.com/news/technology-49893913.

5. Tweet by Elon Musk (@elonmusk), April 5, 2023, https://x.com/elonmusk/status/1643545966811975680.

6. Cade Metz and Ryan Mac, "Tech Leaders Blamed San Francisco for Bob Lee's Killing. Then Came the Arrest," *New York Times*, April 14, 2023, www.nytimes.com/2023/04/14/business/bob-lee-tech-reaction-san-francisco.html.

7. Tweet by Jason Calacanis (@jason), April 7, 2023, https://x.com/Jason/status/1644372960814436354.

8. Cited in Scott Alan Lucas, *Last Night in San Francisco: Tech's Lost Promise and the Killing of Bob Lee* (Steerforth, 2025), 53.

9. Evgeny Morozov, *To Save Everything, Click Here: The Folly of Technological Solutionism* (PublicAffairs, 2014).

10. Tweet by Elon Musk, March 6, 2020, online at https://x.com/elonmusk/status/1236029449042198528.

11. "Silicon Valley Billionaire Tim Draper in Conversation with Art&-Co Founder Bundeep Singh Rangar," *European Business Magazine*, July 10, 2020, online at https://europeanbusinessmagazine.com/uncategorized/silicon-valley-billionaire-tim-draper-conversation-artco-founder-bundeep-singh-rangar/.

12. Jon Passantino, "Elon Musk Says He Sent Ventilators to California Hospitals, They Say They Got Something Else Instead," *CNN Business*, April 17, 2020, online at https://edition.cnn.com/2020/04/17/tech/elon-musk-ventilators-california.

13. Marc Andreessen, "It's Time to Build," April 18, 2020, online at https://a16z.com/its-time-to-build/.

14. Tweet by Elon Musk, May 11, 2020, https://x.com/elonmusk/status/1259945593805221891.

15. Anthony Ha, "Marc Andreessen Reportedly Told Group Chat That Universities Will 'Pay the Price' for DEI," *TechCrunch*, July 12, 2025, online at https://techcrunch.com/2025/07/12/marc-andreessen-reportedly-told-group-chat-that-universities-will-pay-the-price-for-dei/.

Chapter 3

1. Sarah Wynn-Williams, *Careless People: A Cautionary Tale of Power, Greed, and Lost Idealism* (Flatiron Books, 2025).

2. Transcript of *Squawk Box*, July 21, 2025, online at https://www.cnbc.com/2025/07/21/cnbc-transcript-us-treasury-secretary-scott-bessent-speaks-with-cnbcs-squawk-box-today.html.

3. Achille Mbembe, *Necropolitics* (Duke University Press, 2019).

4. Louis Althusser, *On Ideology* (Verso, 2008), 36.

5. Mad Money, CNBC, October 15, 2015. The video can be found at www.youtube.com/watch?v=rGfaJZAdfNE.

6. Veena Dubal, "An Uber Ambivalence: Employee Status, Workers Perspectives, and Regulation in the Gig Economy," in *Beyond the Algorithm: Qualitative Insights for Gig Work Regulation* (Cambridge University Press, 2020), 33–56.

7. Veena Dubal, "The New Racial Wage Code," *Harvard Law and Policy Review* 15, no. 2 (2020): 511–49.

8. Richard Barbrook and Andrew Cameron, "The Californian Ideology," 1995, www.imaginaryfutures.net/2007/04/17/the-californian-ideology-2/.

9. G. W. F. Hegel, *The Phenomenology of Spirit*, trans. A. V. Miller (Oxford University Press, 1977), 118.

10. Tweet by Alex Blechman (@AlexBlechman), November 8, 2021.

11. Angela Nagle, *Kill All Normies* (Zero Books, 2017).

12. One place he made this claims was at the Conservative Political Action Conference (CPAC) in February 2025. The remarks can be viewed at www.youtube.com/watch?v=fPq3WxxCoP4.

Chapter 4

1. Leslie Berlin, *The Man Behind the Microchip: Robert Noyce and the Invention of Silicon Valley* (Oxford University Press, 2006), 87.

2. Joel N. Shurkin, *Broken Genius: The Rise and Fall of William Shockley, Creator of the Electronic Age* (Palgrave Macmillan, 2006), 181.

3. Barbara and John Ehrenreich, "The Professional-Managerial Class," *Radical America* 11, no. 2 (1977): 7–31.

4. Adrian Daub, "The Undertakers of Silicon Valley," *Guardian*, August 21, 2018.

5. Quinn Slobodian, *Hayek's Bastards* (Zone Books, 2025).

6. Rebecca Lewis, "Tech's Right Turn: The Rise of Reactionary Politics in Silicon Valley and Online," PhD diss., Stanford University, 2024. Online at https://purl.stanford.edu/mn544hj9083.

7. Frank Gregorsky's presentation "The Telecosmic Future," given on January 11, 1994, can be found online at www.c-span.org/program/public-affairs-event/the-telecosmic-future/42611.

8. George Gilder, *The Spirit of Enterprise* (Simon and Schuster, 1986), 17.

9. "Is Quality of U.S. Population Declining? Interview with a Nobel Prize–Winning Scientist," *US News and World Report*, November 22, 1965.

10. Charles Murray and Richard Herrnstein, *The Bell Curve: Intelligence and Class Structure in American Life* (Free Press, 1994).

11. Amanda Hess, "What Is Elon Musk's IQ?" *New York Times*, April 5, 2025.

12. "Emphatically agree. Elon Musk is the rightful heir to George Mueller, Wernher von Braun, and George Low. Today's NASA? Preoccupied with checking off its DEI boxes." Tweet by Charles Murray (@charlesmurray) May 24, 2025, https://x.com/charles murray/status/1794254167844012157.

13. Alexandre Kojève, *The Notion of Authority*, trans. Hager Weslati (Verso, 2011).

14. Kojève, *Notion of Authority*, 8.

15. Kojève, *Notion of Authority*, 8.

16. Roland Meyer, "'Platform Realism': AI Image Synthesis and the Rise of Generic Visual Content," *Transbordeur* 9 (2025).

17. George Gilder, *Recapturing the Spirit of Enterprise* (ICS Press, 1992).

18. Oliver Decker, "Narzisstische Plombe und sekundärer Autoritarismus," in Johannes Kiess and Elmar Brähler, eds., *Rechtsextremismus der Mitte und sekundärer Autoritarismus* (Gießen, 2015).

19. Ernst Kantorowicz, *The King's Two Bodies: A Study in Medieval Political Theology* (Princeton University Press, 2016).

20. Michael Lewis, *Going Infinite: The Rise and Fall of a New Tycoon* (W. W. Norton, 2023).

Chapter 5

1. The statement was covered at Fox News and can be found at www.youtube.com/watch?v=f662vUrKFhQ.

2. Paresh Dave and Lauren Goode, "Elon Musk's X Sues Advertisers over Alleged Boycott," *Wired*, August 6, 2024, online at www.wired.com/story/elon-musk-x-twitter-rumble-sue-advertisers/.

3. G. W. F. Hegel, *Elements of the Philosophy of Right* (Cambridge University Press, 1991), 238.

4. Hegel, *Elements*, 238.

5. Hegel, *Elements*, 239.

6. Hegel, *Elements*, 48.

7. Oliver Holmes, "Elon Musk Admits Cheating at Video Games, Chat Transcript Appears to Show," *Guardian*, January 22, 2025, online at www.theguardian.com/technology/2025/jan/22/elon-musk-admits-cheating-at-video-games-chat-transcript-appears-to-show.

8. Elizabeth Freeman, *Time Binds: Queer Temporalities, Queer Histories* (Duke University Press, 2010).

9. Immanuel Kant, *Anthropology from a Pragmatic Point of View* (Cambridge University Press, 2006).

10. Walter Isaacson, *Elon Musk* (Simon and Shuster, 2023), 670.

11. Alex Hanna and Emily M. Bender, *The AI Con: How to Fight Big Tech's Hype and Create the Future We Want* (Harper, 2025).

12. Tyler Cowen, "My Favorite Actress Is Not Human," *Free Press*, October 2, 2025.

13. Zoe Kleinman, "Microsoft Boss Troubled by Rise in Reports of 'AI Psychosis,'" BBC, August 20, 2025, online at www.bbc.com/news/articles/c24zdel5j18o.

14. Mario Bunge, "A General Black-Box Theory," *Philosophy of Science* 30, no. 4 (1963): 346–58.

15. Frank Pasquale, *The Black Box Society: The Secret Algorithms That Control Money and Information* (Harvard University Press, 2015).

16. "When AI Flags the Ruler, Not the Tumor—and Other Arguments for Abolishing the Black Box," *Venture Beat*, March 25, 22021.

Chapter 6

1. Moira Donegan lays out this taxonomy in *In Bed with the Right*, "Episode 6: Perverts, Creeps and Priests!," September 11, 2023, https://open.spotify.com/episode/3zaOViJFIShh8csFJbG93v.

2. Kate Manne, *Entitled: How Male Privilege Hurts Women* (Crown, 2020).

3. Quinn Slobodian, *Hayek's Bastards: Race, Gold, IQ, and the Capitalism of the Far Right* (Zone Books, 2025), 173.

4. Curtis Yarvin, "Principles of the Deep Right," *Gray Mirror*, April 23, 2022, online at graymirror.substack.com/p/principles-of-the-deepright.

5. Jordan S. Carroll, *Speculative Whiteness: Science-Fiction and the Alt-Right* (University of Minnesota Press, 2024).

6. Peter Thiel, "The Education of a Libertarian," *Cato Unbound*, April 13, 2009, online at www.cato-unbound.org/2009/04/13/peter-thiel/education-libertarian/.

7. The episode of *The Joe Rogan Experience* is online at www.youtube.com/watch?v=Jk.ehaEIbdU.

Chapter 7

1. Ellen Pao, *Reset: My Fight for Inclusion and Lasting Change* (Random House, 2017), 80.

2. Kate Manne, *Down Girl: The Logic of Misogyny* (Oxford University Press, 2017), 197.

3. "Google's Ideological Echo Chamber" can be found at https://web.archive.org/web/20170809021151/https://diversitymemo.com/.

4. Sara Ahmed, *On Being Included: Racism and Diversity in Institutional Life* (Duke University Press, 2012), 41.

5. Alice E. Marwick und Robyn Caplin, "Drinking Male Tears: Language, the Manosphere, and Networked Harassment," *Feminist Media Studies* 18 (2018): 543–59.

6. Jordan B. Peterson, *12 Rules for Life* (Random House, 2018), 158.

7. Curtis Yarvin, "Uncle Yarv's Dating Call," *Gray Mirror*, September 6, 2021.

8. Yarvin v. Laurenson, Superior Court of California, County of Alameda, HF 23135875.

9. Jessica Calarco, *Holding It Together: How Women Became America's Safety Net* (Portfolio, 2024).

10. Anna Wiener, *Uncanny Valley: A Memoir*, (MCD, 2020), 108.

11. Wiener, *Uncanny Valley*, 112.

12. Richard Feloni, "5 Books That Inspired Billionaire Elizabeth Holmes," Inc., July 5, 2015, online at www.inc.com/business-insider/t-books-that-inspired-elizabethholmes.html.

13. Zoë Schiffer, Leah Feiger, Vittoria Elliott, et al., "The Story of DOGE, as Told by Federal Workers," *Wired*, September 25, 2025, online at www.wired.com/story/oral-history-doge-federal-workers/.

14. Schiffer, Feiger, Elliott, et al., "The Story of DOGE."

Chapter 8

1. "Traffic is driving me nuts. Am going to build a tunnel boring machine and just start digging." Tweet by Elon Musk, December 17, 2016, online at https://x.com/elonmusk/status/810108760010043392.

2. Vanessa Bates Ramirez, "Elon Musk's Boring Company Finishes First Tunnel for 155 mph Vegas Loop," *Singularity Hub*, February 20, 2020, online at https://singularityhub.com/2020/02/20/elon-musks-boring-company-finishes-first-tunnel-for-155mph-vegas-loop/.

3. Mick Akers, "Officials Aim to Have Vegas Loop Operational by Super Bowl LVIII," *Las Vegas Review-Journal*, October 17, 2022, online at www.reviewjournal.com/local/traffic/officials-aim-to-have-vegas-loop-operational-by-super-bowl-lviii-2659224/.

4. Lee Chong Ming, "Mark Zuckerberg Says He'd Rather Risk 'Misspending a Couple of Hundred Billion' Than Be Late to Superintelligence," *Business Insider*, September 19, 2025, online at https://finance.yahoo.com/news/mark-zuckerberg-says-hed-rather-071144830.html.

5. Douglas Rushkoff, *Survival of the Richest* (W. W. Norton, 2022).

6. Pao, *Reset*, 73.

7. Derek Parfit, *Reasons and Persons* (Oxford University Press, 1984), 454.

8. The interview (May 7, 2025) is available at /www.youtube.com/watch?v=6Em4QyUuLUU.

9. Roger Scruton, "Parfit the Perfectionist," *Philosophy* 89, no. 350 (2014).

10. Giuseppe di Lampedusa, *The Leopard* (Collins and Horvill, 1911), 42.

11. "'We Are Scared': ChatGPT Creator Sam Altman Warns about These Dangers from AI," *Business Today Online*, March 19, 2023.

12. Rob Thubron, "OpenAI CEO Sam Altman Warns That the World Might Not Be Far from 'Potentially Scary' Artificial Intelligence," *TechSpot*, February 21, 2023.

The authorized representative in the EU for product safety and compliance is:
Mare Nostrum Group
B.V Doelen 72
4831 GR Breda
The Netherlands

www.ingramcontent.com/pod-product-compliance
Lightning Source LLC
LaVergne TN
LVHW100922110826
845155LV00036B/50

* 9 7 8 1 5 0 3 6 4 8 3 3 3 *